THE HIGH-PERFORMANCE TALENT ACQUISITION ADVANTAGE

10 CRITICAL ISSUES FACING ORGANIZATIONS WANTING TO SOURCE, ATTRACT AND HIRE TOP TALENT TO CREATE A MAJOR COMPETITIVE ADVANTAGE

Jeremy M. Eskenazi

STAR
STRATEGIC TALENT
ACQUISITION ROUNDTABLE
PRESS

CONTENTS

ABOUT THE AUTHOR

Jeremy Eskenazi is currently the Managing Principal of Riviera Advisors, Inc., a boutique Human Resources consulting firm that he founded in 2001. Riviera Advisors partners with organizations globally to improve and enhance their ability to attract and hire talent. Jeremy draws on more than 25 years of experience and expertise to help companies assess and enhance their talent management systems and processes.

Prior to founding Riviera Advisors, Jeremy served as Vice President, Talent Acquisition for Idealab, the world's premier technology business incubator. Jeremy's role encompassed building and leading a global team in the development and delivery of Recruiting and staffing, college relations, and Executive search services to Idealab's more than 30 network companies.

Jeremy came to Idealab after serving as Director of Talent

Acquisition for Amazon.com. In this role, Jeremy led all Talent Acquisition and Recruiting activities for this high-growth global organization. Later, Jeremy served in the role of Vice President, Strategic Growth, with worldwide responsibilities for all Human Resources activities.

Previously, Jeremy led the global professional staffing functions for all of Universal Studios and the Universal Music Group businesses. In his role as Corporate Director, Workforce Planning & Strategic Staffing for Universal Studios, Inc., Jeremy and his team provided leadership for all of the worldwide professional staffing, workforce planning, internal sourcing, college and community organization relations and recruitment, and Executive recruitment activities within the Universal organization.

Jeremy previously held positions at Heublein, Inc., The Knott's Organization, and several years in Human Resources, recruitment and staffing with Hyatt Hotels Corporation.

Jeremy holds a Bachelor of Science from California State Polytechnic University (Cal Poly Pomona). As a professional member of the prestigious National Speakers Association (NSA), Jeremy speaks to many audiences on the value of the staffing function.

Jeremy is a member of the Institute of Management Consultants–USA (IMC-USA), and holds the Certified Management Consultant (CMC) certification. He is also a member of the Society for Human Resources Management (SHRM), where he recently served on the national Staffing Management Special Expertise Panel and the Workforce Planning Standards Workgroup. Jeremy holds certification as a Senior Professional in Human Resources (SPHR) from the Human Resources Certification Institute. A native of Southern California, now residing in Long Beach, in addition to his professional affiliations, Jeremy is a member of the Pasadena Tournament of Roses Association.

Jeremy can be reached at Jeremy@RivieraAdvisors.com

ACKNOWLEDGEMENTS

Thank you to my team at Riviera Advisors who provided themes and content for many of this book's chapters. We work together as a team to support our global clients, and we spend a great deal of time listening to our client's issues and opportunities and we have incorporated many of those into this book. Thanks to John Carrozza, Brad Loewen, and James Mueller at Riviera Advisors for their insights. A special thanks goes to John Carrozza and Brad Loewen for also helping to edit this book. Over the past several years we have had an outstanding Talent Acquisition Analyst internship program at Riviera Advisors that has really helped us to gain additional insights and research on Talent Acquisition trends in and out of our client's organizations and have helped to contribute to this book's contents. Thanks to the Riviera Advisors Talent Acquisition Analyst Alumni, including Ray Hailey, Melany Jensen, Chris Stringfellow, Seyka Huff, Alyssa Salindong, Regina Kim, Andrew Sandoval, and Crystal Foo.

Thanks also goes out to the many Talent Acquisition, Recruiting, Staffing, and Human Resources professionals who provided insights into the content of this book and its source material. Thanks to the many colleagues, former co-workers, team members, bosses, clients, friends, and family all over the world.

A special thanks goes to my writing and editorial partners. A special thanks to Dianne Tennen for her writing and editing skills.

INTRODUCTION

You are probably reading this book because you are responsible for a team whose main objective is to source, attract, and hire top talent into your organization.

In a global talent landscape that is now the most competitive that it has ever been, your responsibilities and importance to your organization have become critical to its growth and competitiveness.

Do you remember the old days, when you could just place an ad in a newspaper or online, and then great candidates would suddenly appear? It was a simple process back then, primarily because there were a lot less companies looking to recruit the same people.

Fast forward to today, candidates have a lot more choice for which organization they want to join, which means you and your team have to now become a 'high-performance' Talent Acquisition team that ensures your organization recruits top talent and places them into important functions of your business.

A high performing team does not mean using a set of 'best practices' though. Think about it. This assumes that practices are homogenous across industries and organizations. While you may have similarities with organizations that are like yours, it's important to realize the uniqueness of your business. I often have clients that ask about the number of requisitions they should have per Recruiter, and I get asked a lot for the 'best practice' for the cost per hire, or for taking care of candidates. Generally speaking, I hate the idea of 'best practices' because there really is no 'one solution' for everyone to blindly apply. As I said, just because it works for someone else, doesn't mean it will work for you. Let me give you an example:

We had a client in the high-end luxury goods industry. Their business was focused on high-value sales and we started our work together with a standard question, "How many requisitions should each Recruiter have?" I told them it didn't matter because they were Recruiting to a 'class' of multiple new employees that all started at the same time. This client would often have one requisition, but needed 30 new hires in this position, and needed them fast. Another organization might have 20 different requisitions, and that Recruiter is working just as hard, perhaps even harder. This is an example of how a 'best practice' didn't fit for this client – it really depends on type of jobs, Hiring Managers, environment, and geography.

Another client of ours was in the service industry. They were looking to hire many service employees at once through one requisition. Even after following 'best practices' they were struggling to hire. How could this be if they were using best practices? Well, being located in high-cost markets such as Park City, Utah and Santa Barbara, California meant that many people who lived within a reasonable commute of the location would need to live in million dollar or more homes. These people were not interested in the entry-level service roles our client had open, and so we had to take another approach to our Talent Acquisition that addressed cost of living nearby. So, a 'best practice' level of requisitions per Recruiter wouldn't work in this environment. Geography and talent markets can significantly change a practice.

Let's instead call them 'success practices'; ones that have worked at other companies and are worth considering. They may not necessarily be 'best' practices for you. This acknowledges that not every practice fits every organization once you take a closer look. And let's face it, we all want to achieve success.

In a hyper competitive market, as we are in today, your job is to find a significant 'edge'. A lever that you can use to be a step ahead of your competition – because you and I know, the difference between an average candidate and a top one is what makes the difference between winning and losing.

How do I know this?

We have worked with many companies with great consumer brands that you'd image many people want to work for. But, many of these companies unfortunately were known for having horrible candidate experiences. It wasn't intentional of course, the last few years for the

Recruiting industry have been wrought with change. It started in the economic crisis of 2008/9, when many global companies made the decision to drastically reduce the size of their Recruiting function. As hiring continued, the teams left behind were not prepared to take care of the volume of candidates applying for each role. As things improved, there were many organizations that did not fully hire back their Talent Acquisition team as things sped up – and that led to a damaged Employer Brand – which we'll talk about later in this book.

While it should be a priority to improve the candidate experience, it was slow to rebound for some. The industry took notice and actually developed several awards for best candidate experience to help accelerate the transformation back to a place employers could be proud of. We should not need awards to help with this area, but as you can see, it has been a way to shine light on a critical success factor for hiring as teams get built back up.

Never take for granted what a candidate experience can do to your external brand. It's another dimension of remaining on top in this hyper competitive market and requires a strategic focus.

I've decided to write this book to share the insights and strategies that I have learned working with our global clients to help you gain that edge that you are looking for.

By having a deep understanding of the true issues that hold your team back from high-performance Talent Acquisition, you're going to realize there are new strategies you can take action on to give your team their 'edge'.

If this book resonates with you and you'd like a Complimentary Talent Acquisition Strategy Session (Value $1495.00) to discuss how to optimize your Talent Acquisition function to reach your objectives, then reach out to my office at +1-562-856-5787 or visit www.RivieraAdvisors.com/StrategySession

CHAPTER #1

Is your Talent Acquisition team optimized? Are your Talent Acquisition processes optimized for your organization?

The starting point for any high performing team is to look at what, and how they perform their function. When you look at your Talent Acquisition team, do you think you have optimized the function? Are you getting the most you can out of the limited resources available on your team?

Let me explain exactly what I mean by an optimized function. Generally speaking, most Human Resources organizations do not have enough resources to handle all functions, levels, and geographies all the time; generally this is not possible. Therefore, it's important to focus the most critical resources, and specifically, hiring and Recruiting for the most critical jobs. Let's make sure not to get these confused with the requisitions that the loudest and most vocal Hiring Manager has open. These are the roles that are the most difficult, and most important to the business that you fill. This usually means a commercial role, or business development genre.

It could also be roles related to product development and innovation, like design and sales roles that fill the need for talent that helps deliver your product or service (not staff or support roles).

I've often seen small teams tasked with all functions, levels and geographies. This means that in eight hours, one full cycle Recruiter could be scrambling to hire payroll clerks in Mexico, Software Engineers in Turkey, and Salespeople in China. They'll need to know about hiring practices, local laws, cultural differences, and handle all candidate communication.

It seems that someone performing well at these tasks would be very valuable – but I could question whether someone like this exists, and if they can sustain this type of spread. Most full cycle Recruiters will try to cover as much as possible and do they best they can; unfortunately, they fail often. By understanding the business needs and focusing on what is most needed, you create prioritization for your team, and help manage

Is your Talent Acquisition team optimized? Are your
Talent Acquisition processes optimized for your organization?

3

expectations – which we'll talk more about a little later, and is critically important.

Think about your strategy, and how far out have you planned. Is it realistic to create 10 year Talent Acquisition or Human Resource plans anymore? Likely not. Even five years seems unrealistic – these are change-filled times we are in. While your team might have been struggling to be everywhere at every time, it doesn't mean you don't have the right team in place. Many companies do have the talent within to work with agency swiftness and professionalism. Once you, as their leader, ensure the team is optimized, they can continue to be the superstars they all want to be for the organization.

A team of superstars should be focused on the most important tasks. Once you have your high priority hires covered, then you can focus on how you think it will be best to handle the other tasks, perhaps through outsourcing or search firms for example. If you've never evaluated these options, looking at the cost comparison of keeping these functions internal and allowing your high priority tasks lag is far more costly, in both money, and relationships. Remember, the goal is to ensure you are using the generally limited resources you have effectively.

I can appreciate that many of us have those moments where we feel we're working as hard as possible, and are still falling behind. To that, I will remind you that in today's climate, in many companies, Human Resources Executives do not have enough resources. Optimizing your team will make a drastic difference – the ultimate makeover that will also change how you feel about what you can deliver to the business.

From this

To this

It can be difficult to see things from the ground level. Let me give you a few suggestions of what to look for – again, these are 'success practices' – not 'best practices' that you could implement. In addition to not prioritizing

Is your Talent Acquisition team optimized? Are your
Talent Acquisition processes optimized for your organization?

5

the most important tasks, it could also be that you do not have the right type of people for your Talent Acquisition function. There may be a lack of Hiring Manager intake process. Your teams might not have the skills to assess the right candidates correctly or spend too much time on background checks. Some of your Recruiters might only handle sourcing or coordinate scheduling and do paperwork.

Your team must be optimized. From your own perspective, this means managing; coaching, mentoring, directing, and leading. Of the people you manage, if they are not optimized, what you might get are situations like these:

We had been working with a large company in the financial services industry. They had a large group of employees in call centers, and another large group of employees in more traditional office settings. This client took our recommendation to use a segment recruitment approach, meaning, they looked at their segments as high volume, and high skill. They divided their team to have some working on call center hiring only, while others worked to fill the more challenging roles like Analysts and Accountants. In the contact center segment, they used a one-to-many ratio for Recruiting, and a one-to-few ratio for the more skilled type roles. This segment by function type of Recruiting worked really well for them because they took a critical function out of their core team. They removed the administrative part of Recruiting – for them, it was a big time suck and with the resources available on this team, their time was more valuably spent on Recruiting and not doing lots of paperwork, or entering data into an Applicant

Tracking System (ATS). They were able to spend time with candidates and create a better candidate experience for the people they were meeting with.

If you have the resources to internally keep the administrative function within your team, you could transform these employees into a shared services model too. This way the coordinators provide services to the whole team. They can provide shared services and are able to 'follow the sun' for geographical coverage; just what global teams need, 'always on' support.

At times, Human Resources teams are approved to hire more resources to help keep up with volume and group the function. This is always an exciting moment – it seems like the white flag of hope - your team will finally be unburdened. I want to caution you all that we have seen several significant failures when this happens. Simply hiring when your Hiring Managers complain they have too many requisitions open, or for too long isn't necessarily the solution. The challenge actually might be solved by the shared service model I just shared with you. It's a way to optimize your team that keeps the right people doing the right work at the right times. More people doesn't automatically equal an improved function.

Every team is different, so be sure to really look at what is best for your team. What you should insource and outsource needs to be looked at from many dimensions. I'll go into more detail in future chapters, for now, I'll share that for a Recruiter, you can expect the same cost internally versus externally to hire.

Is your Talent Acquisition team optimized? Are your
Talent Acquisition processes optimized for your organization?

7

An optimized team is the foundation for your success, and with your house in order from the start, you can move into other important areas. **An optimized team is able to improve hiring speed, hiring quality, and cost, all while improving stakeholder relationships and satisfaction – for Hiring Managers and candidates.**

So let's assume you have the right people, performing the right functions on your team. This covers the 'what', the next question is 'how' they are performing the functions. Do you think your systems and processes are efficient?

We can likely all agree that there are many options when you're looking at systems and processes. The key is having the right mix of tools and being clear on process, so that you can deliver a consistent and properly measured function through your optimized team.

Generally, where I see process issues is when an organization has some sort of urban mythology – for example - there has to be something on a particular type of paper, and if it's not on that paper, we'll get in trouble.

We once had a client in a very heavily regulated industry. This led them to be quite risk averse, and part of their culture was to triple check everything. While thorough, it slowed down many processes. They would print every single document for all Recruiting activity, including corresponding emails with candidates, forms, and background screening materials. Each Recruiter had a cardboard box for each candidate and each job. They would fill these boxes, then send them to corporate records where it would be stored for 10 years. In addition to killing a lot of trees, wasting time walking to printers, and properly recycling ink drums, I asked them how many times they go back to the files. Not surprisingly, the answer was very rarely.

Organizations spend a lot more time on the exception, instead of what actually happens. It's the 80/20 rule, if you can focus on managing against what actually happens 80% of the time, you'll be in much better shape to help your team make the most of their time. Let's not forget that there is a cost value to each activity we decide to take on. Ask yourself if your team is focused on what actually happens the majority of the time.

Processes in an organization versus practices in Recruiting should also be looked at from a 'success factor' perspective, not a 'best practice' view. Some organizations view this as a road through the mountains and enjoy the journey. Others set high guard rails, meaning that Hiring Managers can get into less trouble because there are more rules. However, as we saw with working to the exception, you spend a lot time fighting what might not happen. Assume the mistakes will be the exceptions and try not to be too rigid in your processes.

I'll share with you a story of a client who had high guard rails. We've had clients who take things too far in one direction, and also the other. One of our clients had a Human Resources leader who was extremely distrustful of technology and was vehemently against ATSs. He had his coordination team enter relevant information into a home-grown solution through online resume submissions. This process was heavily administrative and the available information for Hiring Managers varied greatly because of the individuals performing the tasks. It was not only a time suck, but the process was painful for the employees as well.

Another client of ours was keen to have candidates kept up to date as often as possible. Candidate communication is fantastic and should be a priority, however, this process stated that both the Recruiter and the Coordinator were providing almost daily updates to desirable candidates, even if there was nothing to update. Candidates who took a survey a few months later shared that the over-communication without any direction was a deterrent from wanting to join the company and seemed inefficient.

Both organizations were able to find better paths, but it's easy to fall into inefficient processes that make sense at the time you set them up. Part of our role is to be able to assess what is working, what isn't, and have an ear to the ground on ways to make what we do better. I've heard many tales of processes that just didn't make sense, and yet people would cling to them as if the apocalypse would come if anything changed. We often require our teams to change, be agile and adjust to business needs, so make sure you're in a position to do that as well. Or it becomes difficult to expect it of others, right?

Where I net it out is that there is a balance of technology and human touch that still exists today. Like many ecosystems, if you find the right harmony, you will allow the community to flourish.

A lot of times, where I see serious problems of a process sucking valuable time is when an organization finds an ATS that has all bells and whistles, but then the organizational process insists on specific customization. They try to make the system fit their process, but the system can't do it, there is a manual work around – and it's a time suck. Clients need help to understand that the tool is not too different than say an accounting or financial software. In corporations we have 'GAAP' (Generally Accepted Accounting Principles) – which means there is a standardized process for using it – but we don't have the same in Talent Acquisition. So the Talent Acquisition software companies build tools for highly varied organizations and they don't match well together. If you want a simplified process or a change to the system, don't tell the system to get into your process – don't force square peg into a round hole.

Is your Talent Acquisition team optimized? Are your
Talent Acquisition processes optimized for your organization?

11

To sum up, the Talent Acquisition advantage is having an optimized team firing on all cylinders that gets you improved speed, quality, and cost with the same amount of resources.

CHAPTER #2

How Can You Build A Stronger Relationship Between Your Talent Acquisition Team and Your Hiring Managers?

Let's assume your Talent Acquisition team is firing on all cylinders. Your processes are flawless, and your systems are running smoothly. With these elements in place, one might assume that your time to fill, quality of candidates, and retention numbers are doing well too – but they unfortunately are not.

When you start examining why this could be, it surfaces that some of the feedback from the Hiring Managers at the company is not positive. They want candidate options faster, they want to reduce time to fill, and they want to pay less for their hires.

Does this interaction sound like a familiar exchange between your team and the Hiring Managers at your organization?

Here is an important bit of information: Hiring Managers may not always know how to be good partners. No, I'm not passing the buck or villainizing them in our own defense. It's more of an epidemic that comes from companies viewing Talent Acquisition as a service that is provided to the business, instead of a two-way relationship. There are two parties coming to the table and they BOTH have specific goals. If the Hiring Managers don't come to the table as a partner, how can they expect to have fantastic long-term hires that meet their business needs?

As Human Resources or Talent Acquisition leaders inside organizations, not only do we need to provide development tools and resources to the Talent Acquisition team, but we need to provide the same to Hiring Managers to make them more effective. They are responsible for our Talent Acquisition at the end. As professionals, it's our job to give them a better set of tools.

Hiring Managers are often taught that if they apply pressure, escalate their displeasure, or start making candidate suggestions themselves, they will see better results. While communication and ongoing dialogue is important, the approach of the dialogue is often all wrong.

Have you heard your Hiring Managers ask for high volumes of resumes quickly? They often have a mindset that sounds something like, "If the Recruiter sends me enough resumes, I will find the right one myself." This of course is false more often than it's accurate – we all have stories of the lack of fit in resumes when we send blanket or generic job descriptions out. Some of the resumes that come across our desks are so far off what we are looking for ... it's laughable.

While Recruiters are looking for quality, fit, and qualifications – all elements we are trained to be able to separate so our Hiring Managers are only looking at suitable candidates, Hiring Managers can often be distracted by 'shiny objects', whatever those might be on a given resume. So with their lack of training on how to be a great partner, they are often unfairly hard on the Talent Acquisition team they look to as servants who provide customer service. Do any of these sound familiar?

"I don't get enough resumes."

"My Recruiter doesn't ask the right questions."

"This is taking too much time."

"They don't know my business to get me the right candidates."

"They don't know how my business operates, they just push paper."

When Recruiters have to reply directly to these requests and demands, they are not allowed the opportunity to add value to their Hiring Manager's business. Imagine how much more value the Hiring Manager who sees their Talent Acquisition partner as a consultant and trusted advisor receives. In this desirable arrangement, the Talent Acquisition partner can make suggestions, put together a sourcing strategy, and push back when a Hiring Manager's request is unreasonable or their expectations haven't been well managed.

A Recruiter who pushes resumes around is not effective in their role. You can tell when your team starts to get overwhelmed because they start to look for ways to cut corners when they are too busy. Maybe they cave and just send 500 resumes to the Hiring Manager, or continue to push the same requisition to the same job boards without results, just to check a box that says they are still actively looking to fill the open role. When this happens, you can be sure that the Hiring Managers will start to complain and start to invent their own solutions – usually sans any direct target or strategy.

What can Recruiters do to avoid getting into this situation? They need to do a really good job **setting and managing expectations**.

If the Recruiter can't do this, nothing else in a functioning relationship will be possible. It's as simple as having a conversations that sounds like, "This is what I will do, this is what you will do", then setting up the timelines and ensuring there is clear accountability. The Hiring Manager cannot simply show up and say "I need this type of candidate" and have a go-fetch attitude. There is a mutual, vested interest in finding the right candidate for the long term – perhaps an even bigger interest on the part of the Hiring Manager. It's important they understand their role from the start to avoid toxic relationships.

It reminds me of a time a Hiring Manager called me to complain about a Recruiter assigned to their business group. They wanted to know if they could schedule a status update every morning at 8am. In this meeting, they wanted to review all newly received resumes from the night before. The Recruiter of course supported 12-15 other Hiring Managers, so these meetings were creating a huge problem. The Recruiter had not set any expectations on the amount of time, when the Hiring Manager would receive resumes, how often, and the actions for each side once those resumes were received. The Recruiter agreed to the meetings initially, but it did not help the relationship at all. We helped them fix it by re-setting expectations with the Hiring Manager and delivering what we agreed to: one package of resumes once a week that had been vetted by an expert, and twice weekly status updates.

Another client of ours had an eager Hiring Manager who decided he wanted to go splashy with advertising his open positions. He didn't feel he was receiving enough resumes, so one weekend, he went to a football game and came back on Monday and shared his brainstorm with his Recruiter. "We should use the Goodyear blimp with an ad that says to call me directly if interested, which will attract more leads than you've been able to send me." We started to examine why a Hiring Manager might make this sort of suggestion. A Hiring Manager fielding calls from an ad that over 20,000 people might see seemed ludicrous. Was it really that the volume was low and this was the only solution, or was there something more?

We discovered the root cause pretty quickly. It turns out the Recruiter didn't set expectations on their sourcing strategy. The Hiring Manager assumed that if they didn't receive mountains of resumes quickly, that the Recruiter was doing nothing to help them. We set up an intake meeting with the Hiring Manager to outline the strategy and let them know what was being done.

Of course, we didn't want to shut down the Goodyear blimp idea that the man was clearly so excited about. We did the work to find out the cost and came back to the Hiring Manager within a few days. It turns out that the blimp costs $60,000 per MINUTE, with a minimum purchase of 5 minutes. Even if someone was going to approve the $100,000's spend (before any additional costs), the next available space was 12 weeks away – so not a great sourcing tactic on many fronts.

What we were able to share with the Hiring Manager was that the last five people hired from his department were found on university alumni job boards and through employee referrals. So we sourced the appropriate target job boards, and created a special employee referral program to encourage his team to help us fill the roles. He was much more comfortable after learning this information, and the Recruiter was able to gain back some credibility and work to rebuild the partnership.

What went right in that story? First and foremost, transparency in the process. Right after the meeting, the Recruiter was able to use their magic 'mojo' to get great candidates right away. But the sourcing strategy is often not shared with the Hiring Manager and you see what happens when there is a misconception that the Recruiter isn't a strategic advisor.

You may be thinking that it would be great to have this type of relationship between your Hiring Managers and Recruiters, but the damage is already done in some cases. Fear not! A turnaround story can happen, it is not an urban myth! There are a few things to remember to mount this comeback endeavor into the Hiring Manager's good graces again.

It starts with an intake meeting. You simply cannot develop a great relationship with a Hiring Manager without an intake session. The Recruiter cannot assume each requisition is the same as it previously was, even if it's similar to a past one. Their job is to listen. You cannot talk about unforeseen challenges, or expectations without a conversation. Each search should have its own intake session no matter what. Even if you know the Hiring Manager and have a good relationship already. Keep a checklist of questions you want to ask for each session, or send them in advance for the Hiring Manager to be able to think about. Set expectations after the intake meeting by sending something that feels like a service level agreement – without being a formal one. It will outline the discussion and who will do what, when. Include the actions the Hiring Manager must take if you're to be successful as a team.

Be sure to meet with Hiring Manager in person

We understand not all relationships can be fixed that easily. We once had a client who was experiencing the bad relationship blues. To help them rebuild the bridge, they were provided with a process to provide consistency and be crystal clear about expectations. It looked something like this:

1. Use a template for your Hiring Manager intake meetings.

2. Follow up after the meeting with an email outlining everything you will do, and everything the Hiring Manager will do, and how you will achieve your plan together.

It got very specific, even to the level of:

To fill a job fast, the Hiring Manager has to reply within 24 hours of receiving resumes.

Immediately, we started to see improvements that made the working relationship much more effective. The Hiring Manager understood expectations and partnered to set a shared course of action. Both also felt more confidence in the accountability they each held and it allowed the Recruiter to show their reliability. This is what turned the relationship around.

In this digital age, you might be tempted to automate the intake process. I want to encourage you – strongly – not to let this process become impersonal. Relationships matter, and the intake meeting is a key opportunity to set the tone early and be sure about how the working relationship will progress. Email has proven to be a boon and bust for relationships. Don't let your intake process become a sterile checklist - it could backfire if the nuances of each role aren't shared. You'd be surprised what people remember during the free flow of human-to-human conversation. A phone call can be effective as well if geography or schedules prove to be a challenge, but do not allow your Recruiters and Hiring Managers to avoid all human interaction.

That covers the Recruiter and Human Resources accountability, but it takes two to tango. The Hiring Managers cannot be passive in this process and expect top results. After all, the candidates found for them will be part of their team, drive the culture they produce, and help deliver results for the Hiring Manager's team.

The role of the Hiring Manager is important —and it's especially important that they understand their role. It's a really good thing when they want to take on more, and have an active interest in where their candidates are coming from. There are occasions when the Hiring Managers' take on too much though. It should be their job to get involved, not to take over. They are not in the role of Recruiter or Human Resources because they are not the experts when it comes to many things, including compliance issues. As an example, if a Hiring Manager receives a resume by bypassing the Recruiter, it could be trouble for the whole organization if a regulatory audit occurs and resumes aren't being tracked centrally.

With role clarity and accountabilities in place, the teams will be better set up for success. The overarching theme in the relationship is communication. Being transparent, open, and clear about what you are working on, and the progress and status of hires-to-plan, will only add to the relationship and confidence in the Talent Acquisition team.

Our goal is always to have great partnerships between Recruiters and Hiring Managers. Recruiters have great experience and are able to find and assess the best candidates. If the relationships are positive and your Hiring Managers are still reporting that they are not seeing quality talent presented to them, then you might have the wrong people in the wrong roles.

Setting and managing expectations is the key.

CHAPTER #3

How Can Your Talent Acquisition Organization Leverage Your Employer Brand To Attract And Not Repel Candidates?

We talked a little bit about what a bad Employer Brand can do to your company in Chapter 2. Let's circle back there for a moment and get on the same page about this wildcard.

An Employer Brand is what employees and candidates say about your company and the work experience when you're not in the room. It's not something you can go out and buy, or have a fancy branding exercise to develop and replace if you don't like the one you have. By definition, branding is a means of identifying and differentiating a company, a product, or a service. Branding includes the tangible and intangible features, services, and benefits that create and influence an ongoing relationship. It is the development of an affinity for a product that in turn, takes on elevated meaning and a predisposition to buy or join. A brand is a set of convictions that surrounds a product, service or job in the consumer's (job seeker/ employees) mind. Effective branding creates a sustainable competitive advantage. Negative branding can damage your ability to reach your goals.

Remember, you do not create it. What you can create is your Employer Brand message. The positioning you want to be affiliated with, and the things you stand for as an employer. However, if you don't live up to them, well – some of you know how that turns out.

If you're not sure what your Employer Brand is, you need to find out soon. For the US, Canada and parts of Europe, Glassdoor.com is like the Yelp of Employer Branding and can give you a feel for what people are saying. If you're not familiar with the concept of these sites, it's a user-driven website that encourages people to record their experiences with the company, vendor, or merchant. They can write whatever they want, even if it's negative and they can encourage people to stay far far away. The flip side is that reviewers can also sing your praises and wax lyrical about you. The warning I'll give when you review this is that it's not 100% effective. The reason is very logical, think about the last time you filled out a survey. You were either delighted with something, or were very upset. The same thing applies for employees, former employees, and candidates, so you tend to see wild swings of positive or negative comments. These are generally the most active people on Employer Branding sites.

Since the average person only takes action if they are feeling extreme, you might be wondering how to measure people in the middle. You'll want to measure them regularly and have an accurate picture.

Start with an environmental scan. Brand expression can often be found in a variety of media. Whether it's print, video, social media, etc. you will quickly get a sense of how people view an organization. Of course, from the company side, they will be very slick and marketing-driven materials. Don't be fooled by the 'shiny object' – the general public and your desired candidate pool won't be.

Not good.

The ones that look authentic are more believable and effective. Perhaps you've seen a great website with quotes from people who are not photo-shopped beyond belief. Maybe it was a great set of employee-produced videos where they are talking about their personal experience of working at the company. It could even be a campaign that runs in local subway stations that authentically represent your brand. You get the idea – it's about your brand, and the image that is projected across platforms. Whatever you choose, make sure it is authentic.

While actors and models do really well in the entertainment field, remember, your Employer Brand is not entertainment. Having employees represent the Employer Brand you want to have will give them a voice, before someone interacts with your company. It can be part of an Employee Advocacy Program – but most important is that it syncs up with your consumer brand. Imagine you have a great product to work with and your employees can only talk about how difficult or unfair it is to work for you.

As the head of the Human Resources or Talent Acquisition function, there are a few things you can do to influence the Employer Brand. First and foremost, know that the Employer Brand is for your company. This means both what your aspirations are, and what your actual Employer Brand is – even if it's not optimal at the moment. You own the Employer Brand message, so if it needs a reset, this is an activity for you to push forward, but it should never be done as a solo mission. You should partner with your Communication and Marketing teams and leverage their expertise.

An Employer Brand is not necessarily changed overnight, but every time you interact with a candidate, you create an impression. When the Recruiting process is over the candidate may walk away thinking, "Wow, what a great company—if they had another opening I'd apply there again." Or the candidate may think, "What a bunch of jerks. I'd never want to work there."

Now multiply these impressions dozens or even hundreds of times. This is a powerful force. This is your professional brand and your opportunity to create the first experience.

I've heard some misguided folks say things like "I don't worry about the Employer Brand, our company is coveted." And things of that nature. Whether you want to believe this or not though, the fact is, you have no choice but to care. With every candidate interview you are *creating* your brand; you just may not be *managing* your brand. Pick your favorite consumer brand – or one you'd love to work for. Now imagine you read and heard multiple reports about a terrible employee experience. Perhaps their managers reduce people to tears, or they don't deliver adequate pay or benefits in the eyes of their employees. Would you second guess your desire to work there?

Let's look at how to manage the Employer Brand. I suggest taking the messages that best focus what you are, where you want to go, who will help you get there, and how they will do so. Those messages then need to be communicated and cemented into all that is shared with people – both internally and externally. If you do it well, you'll be able to achieve some goals that Employer Brands help with. Goals like:

- ✓ *Expressing the nature of your company.*

- ✓ *Differentiating you from competitors.*

- ✓ *Working across all forms of communication.*

- ✓ *Working within the overall company brand.*

- ✓ *Adding value to the overall brand.*

- ✓ *Getting the right candidates into your pipeline.*

- ✓ *Gaining respect and building morale from employees already employed.*

Think about the things you have to work with in order to manage your Employer Brand. Your company name, logo, and other trademarks, and the individual brands of products and services offered all contribute. It's the general sense of the work environment and the public perception of the company. Many companies consider affiliating themselves with a celebrity to try and drive a perception of their brand. Athletes, actors, and even social media influencers have been hired to help with this (the caution of course is if this person's behavior suddenly doesn't align with your desired brand, you are now tied to them). The people, symbols, and meaning we try to attribute to the company can be a powerful tool in communicating where the organization is headed.

The brand management process is how brand development proceeds from the first task—asset assessment—through five stages, to emerge as the organizations' brand expression in the marketplace. These five tasks are:

1. **Asset Assessment**. Be honest: what are your strengths and weaknesses? How large is your company—do you need people who thrive in an intense corporate environment or do you want people who are happy to have a more stable career? What benefits do you offer? Is there opportunity for advancement?

2. **Employee Involvement**. What is your organizational culture? Is it vertical, with top-down direction with little front-line input, or are decisions made on a broad collaborative basis? Is there opportunity for creative thinking?

3. **Competitive Assessment**. What other organizations can your candidates work for? You need to know who

your competitors are and what they offer. If another company offers higher wages, can you compensate with profit sharing or better benefits?

4. **Brand Positioning**. You need to know where your organization fits in the overall market. Does your company compete on price, like Walmart, or are you targeting the upscale market? Are you known for promoting from within? Does your company have a reputation for treating women and minorities fairly?

5. **Brand Expression**. This is the combined result of all of the 'brand signals' that are present in the marketplace and are picked up by consumers and candidates. Every element of your Employer Brand needs to be in alignment. For example, if you claim to provide equal opportunity for every race, creed, and gender, you'd better make sure that candidates who walk into your offices see employees of different races, creeds, and genders.

For the consultative Recruiter, the mission is to fill the organizational pipeline with qualified candidates. What do you have to work with? The answer depends upon the combination of everything that goes into the brand management process. Let me share an example of a well-managed Employer Brand.

A client of ours creates and operates pioneering technology companies. They wanted to create a brand management process that expresses the nature of their organization and differentiates their product and services from their competitors. They wanted to work across all media and really focus on employee input. We started with internal focus groups with cross sections of employees - technical, non-technical, new hires, old-timers, different levels of employees, and various geographies – to hear how they described the company.

Their brand assets and employee feedback let them know they had a decent Employer Brand already. With highlights like a good work environment and a unique compensation menu, employees shared that they tended to naturally advocate for the company. The focus groups also revealed information about where people had come from, what had prompted them to leave elsewhere, and what they were looking for. The most fruitful discussion for this client was how joining the company measured against their expectations, and what would keep them there.

It was learned that *in other companies* where staff had worked, the work was boring, staff were underpaid, underappreciated, underutilized, treated like 'peons' with too many 'suits', and had unpleasant managers. There was an overall feeling of disenfranchisement. Outside of the company, there was a disconnect between anything they did, and anything that happened.

The client had already positioned themselves as a company where there was responsibility, respect, empowerment, and trust. *The opportunity to make things happen* became the Employer Brand positioning. The branding campaign built on top of the positioning would have to expand upon the themes of responsibility and empowerment expressed in the tagline; retain a clean and orderly appearance to work within the brand and to reflect the order of thinking, and break through the clutter of standard promises, bulleted facts, and self-conscious attempts to look hip.

They created a campaign and the tagline became the obligation to make something happen. It was geographically relevant, and it left space for individual initiative and imagination, while directly connected to the success of the client's positioning.

In today's competitive global economy, even during periods of high unemployment when there is a surplus of active candidates, woe unto the Recruiter who takes his or her job for granted.

Your professional goal is twofold: to place the best possible candidate in every open position, and to ensure that your pipeline is producing a steady stream of qualified candidates. To do this — especially when the economy heats up and unemployment rates go down — your organization must create and manage two sets of brands: your company's external brand in the minds of potential candidates, and the internal brand of your Talent Acquisition team.

The way you imagine people see you

How they actually see you

This requires a high level of professionalism and ethics in how you interact with your individual candidates (both those whom you hire and those whom you do not hire), and how you interact with the company and its Executives and Hiring Managers.

We live in a 360-degree world of relationships. It's important that all relationships are nurtured and positive. Don't forget about any of your stakeholders. The list is long at times and includes (but is not limited to); your pool of job candidates, Human Resources Generalists in your company, Hiring Managers, Executives, and third-party Recruiters. Some of these relationships may seem competitive or even adversarial; in others, you hold power that you must use wisely. In every case, openness, high ethical standards, and a positive attitude will help with your contribution to your Employer Brand.

Remember, you can't make an Employer Brand. An advertising agency can't help you create a brand. They can help create a *brand message*. Whether or not you know what your brand is isn't the issue. Make sure you know what the themes are that people use to talk about your organization. Then you can manage the expression of the brand – through your Employer Value Proposition, through your goals, vision, and values, and the taglines that best explain what your company is about.

Your Employer Brand cannot be solely aspirational – it has to be accurate for where your organization is today. When your position is too aspirational, people will likely be unhappy when they encounter you – both candidates and employees. If you were in their position, don't you think you'd feel let down too?

CHAPTER #4

How Do You Effectively Attract Diversity Into Your Organization?

Is your team diverse?

Do you invest to ensure your team reflects the needs and attitudes of your customers and clients? They need to reflect the communities your employees live, work in, and provide services to.

I always keep two 'diversities' in mind; Big D and Little D. Big D relates to different people, thoughts, background, geography, experiences. The other, Little D, reflects things like ethnicity, sex, age. While both are important, you must make sure you are focused on the first kind I've described.

It's important because when you're missing these elements inside your organization, everyone thinks the same way, and new ideas, new ways to problem solve, and innovation are all stunted. When you have employees who only follow the boss, the only ideas you have are from that one boss.

There is an element of workplace cultures called Constructive Conflict. If you have good diversity, you should encourage this within your organization. This means there can be open discussion of opposing opinions, and that everyone gets something positive out of it. Everyone shouldn't always be expected to agree with the boss, or nothing will ever change. You want diverse talent in your organization, and you need it on your team. Think about the last time there was a constructive discussion at your team meeting. What did you get out of it, and would you have arrived where you did had there not been Constructive Conflict?

Here's a story for you from my experience. I was working with a national consumer products company, mostly made up of Sales and Marketing talent. Roles like, Brand Managers and Account Representatives were common for this organization. When it came to hiring new people, they were so focused on landing revenue that they decided to only hire people who were similar to their current top performers.

Where would they find these types of people, you might be wondering? Well, they went to college campuses and looked for the sports teams, or members of the university Greek system (Fraternities and Sororities). Although this wasn't their stated strategy, they were looking for outgoing, friendly, Caucasian men (and a few women), who were not the smartest or best in their class, but well liked. As long as they were good looking, outgoing and motivated, the company assumed these would be the next generation of top performers since this had seemingly worked before.

The Talent Acquisition team went on to target second tier schools to ensure they would be a bigger fish in a smaller pond. They spent time schmoozing the candidates, talking to them about what it would be like to sell to grocery stores and be a top performer.

They even applied a selection methodology that invited the current top performers to interview the candidates and have a role in the selection process. Perhaps not shockingly, the current employees LOVED the selected candidates, who were very similar in character.

After a few months in their new jobs, many of the new group quit or were fired for poor performance. They were assigned to inner-city accounts, which were predominately led by ethnically diverse customers. The new hires had a difficult time building relationships with people who were not like they were and thus, were not successful in their roles.

In addition to finding the right candidates, diversity brings several important things to your organization. Here are a few to think about:

1. It helps your Employer Brand. You'll be able to reach a much broader market. And people are attracted to this, especially when they see there are people like them inside the organization. This is another reason to make sure you are authentic. Like showing real employees in your campaign materials as we talked about in

Chapter 3.

2. It shows you are a progressive company. People can see that you spend time and money on diversity. It's obvious from their first encounter with you.

3. The younger generation values diversity. Actually, I'll qualify that – almost everyone values diversity, however, Millennials are much more vocal in what matters to them in a workplace.

4. It can broaden your network. Diverse people who enjoy working at your company will introduce you and advocate for you in their circles.

Not only is hiring for diversity the right thing to do, there are some regulatory requirements that you have to consider as well. In many countries and regions, from North America, to much of Europe, to Australia and New Zealand, there are laws in place that help improve and optimize organizations. Not all organizations have to follow these laws, for example, there are laws for organizations that sell to the United States Government. It requires them to submit an affirmative action plan to improve diversity at the organization and provide updates during the term of the contract. There is also an audit process that ensures that organizations are keeping to their plans.

As another example, in Europe, some countries require other categorical plans for their hiring. A client of ours in France had to submit goals to regulators in order to gain a government contract. They were asked to improve their gender and disability hiring so that there were more females and people with special needs represented by a marked percentage increase each year.

In the UK we had another client who focused on hiring women, and more employees over the age of 50. As you can see, it really depends on the local regulations and what the laws say. In the end, none of the laws say you have to be diverse and it looks like 'this', but there is guidance given in some areas.

There is an exception though, and that will come up if you take a tax break for doing business in a specific country. For example, if a business headquartered in Canada, opened an office in Singapore and wanted to hire 5,000 people, the government in Singapore could stipulate that the company will only receive the tax break if they hire 40% Singaporean nationals.

Don't let regulations drive your diversity efforts. The best way to improve diversity is to be truthful. Don't publish happy smiling employees, hire actors to show up at Recruitment events, or use false testimonials.

A large international restaurant chain used to consistently be top in its class. Unfortunately, they had an issue with retaining their African American employees. They thought hiring an African American Recruitment Manager would attract more diverse hires and thus help them to retain their workforce. It was sort of a chicken before the egg moment. If you want to have better diversity, it takes more than one hire – it has to be a mindset. This chain, despite its top consumer brand, lost its credibility within its Employer Brand and African American candidates didn't want to work for them. They were able to change over time with a lot of hard work.

Beyond any legalities, you can see that a focus on diversity is the right thing to do. It's good for your employees, it's good for your brand, and it's good for your organization. Try not to approach this type of hiring as just a metric as it will show – much like you can see when other's approaches are disingenuous.

If you approach this as a metric, you could end up like a client of ours. They were so focused on diversity metrics that they produced a whole book on it. They toiled over this book for hours – it had every type of diversity metric possible to measure in it. The issue – after all these hours and all their efforts to encourage people to use it, it fell flat. It was too specific, too limiting in the options to hire, and much too rigid for a people measurement. The team needed to re-optimize their time after this experience, and rebuild trust that they were hiring for the right reasons.

While there is no 'one size fits all' playbook for diversity – there are types of talent you will want on your team. You can go about hiring them in different ways, but I will share some 'success practices' with you that might be helpful.

Referral programs. If you have great talent on your team who are highly engaged and doing a great job, they likely have similar friends. Consider offering incentives with longer retention pay out times to ensure your team is helping attract people who are a good fit. You can also have them act as ambassadors in alumni groups or clubs they are a part of.

Campus strategy. Of course you don't want to be like our client who only scoped second tier Greek systems and athletic programs, however, a strong campus strategy is a great way to help create a diverse team because you can more easily target diversity on a university campus. Setting up early career development programs is also good for your Employer Brand, and ensures your talent can develop with your business.

Cultural awareness training for Hiring Managers. We know that this group needs your help to build relationships. Your professional expertise can also help them look for areas of opportunity within their teams. Identifying unconscious bias is an area of learning and development that has taken off in recent years and has been effective in many organizations.

Workplace preparedness. It is one thing to say you want diversity – setting up your physical space and your benefits program to accommodate it is another. Does your office have things like nursing stations? Do you offer extended Maternity/Paternity Leave, and are your Human Resources policies inclusive for Gay, Lesbian, Transgender, etc. people? Do you have prayer rooms facing the correct direction, do your gyms have areas that are exclusive for women? How is your pay equity based on gender?

When it comes to diversity, remember there are two important kinds. It's not enough to have just one, or promote that you care about all, but are really not so interested. The truth always comes out. Give your organization the best competitive advantage you can by helping them find all types of diversity and appreciating all that it brings to the table.

CHAPTER #5

Are You Getting The Executive Support And Buy-In That You Need?

You might be thinking, "The Executives like me, I'm sure I have their support". This is not what I mean when I talk about Executive Support. Talent Acquisition inside a company is a competitive advantage. You know this, and I know this, the question is, do the top leaders of your company know this, and are they committed to using every advantage they have? The CEO, and everyone at the C-level need to have the attitude that if they have the right people, at the right time, in the right place – the company will win!

Having their support to make Talent Acquisition a priority is important. Let me differentiate, as a process, Talent Acquisition is everyone's job. Everyone at the company is accountable to ensure a good candidate experience. This means that everyone is living the desired Employer Brand, and that they manage internal talent properly.

As a function, they are looking to you to ensure it is managed well and that you are making available every aspect of this competitive edge. You need your Senior Leadership Team to understand that the Talent Acquisition function is not some administrative process that creates barriers to hiring. It's not just a Human Resources activity – it's a shared accountability that you and your team ensure is optimized to help the company win.

Sadly there are a lot of Talent Acquisition teams that don't have Executive support. Talent Acquisition and Recruiting are a cost and some leaders see the function as a pure expense, and not an investment. There are lots of technology organizations, and universities who almost always have a statement about how important their people are in their annual reports. They publically talk about how important it is to hire and retain great people. They talk about their investment, and their ambition to spend whatever it takes to get and keep the best people.

While other industries and companies may say the same things, they don't always make it a reality. Some organizations even go so far as to disagree with statements like these. Companies like this likely have less Executive support, hence, their hands are tied when it comes to really investing in top people and using their Talent Acquisition team as strategic advisers. These are also the companies who do not mean it when they say, "People are our greatest assets."

Take a moment to think about your organization. Does your Executive team make statements like this, and do you believe them?

The kind of support that is needed is often more difficult to get – especially if you don't have it today. You can see when there is no Executive support and it results in challenges for the Talent Acquisition function. For example, a company in the service industry said they valued their people. However, in their franchise-driven business model, it hadn't been reported as a great place to work. In fact, their public Employer Brand was pretty terrible. The individual owners were too focused on the bottom line – every hire was seen as a body to fill a role – and one that could be easily replaced if it didn't work out.

This company decided to outsource all of their Talent Acquisition functions to a third party Recruitment Process Outsourcing (RPO) vendor. The RPO's process looks something like – post the job on their website, have candidates put in their application, have someone in a call center contact the candidate and ask basic impersonal questions, type the responses in the system and try to get off the phone. The candidate hears a lot of click click click and when they interject to try and ask a few questions about the role, or the location, the interviewer cannot answer any of them – they are often sitting in an office at the other end of the country and have never visited the location. Ultimately, this company was looking for the cheapest talent, they were not interested in investing in them, and they made Talent Acquisition a low priority.

Let me offer some suggestions on how you might gain more support from your Executives. You are the Chief Human Resources Officer, or the Head of Human Resources. You have to be a champion of the function and be able to communicate the value of your team. From the Senior Leadership's perspective, they may not always see what your team is doing behind the scenes – much of the work your team does is what good partners consider 'the magic'. The ability to get things done and meet the business objective. So how have you been communicating 'the magic' that creates a competitive edge?

Remind them *that whomever has the best people comes out the winner – Executives are aware of this – make sure they know it carries over into their talent.*

*Make sure **everyone knows it**, and believes it.*

Speak their language *and be sure to sell. What is important to the CFO, CMO, Chief Commercial Officer? What tools and reports do they use? You use reports too, make sure they are similar to the tools your counterparts use to get on the same page.*

I've talked to many Human Resources leaders who are not sure how to quantify what they bring to the table. To them, I offer this; you are running a business like any other group. You have the same amount of data and success stories to share, so be sure to package it well. Talk about the business reasons for Talent Acquisition support and investment and again, remind them that the competitive advantage wins.

If you do this well, the rewards will be endless for your team. You know you have buy-in when the CEO and C-level teams show respect for the function by actually following the process themselves. For the jobs that report to them, for the requisitions they want to open, they will be great partners with the Talent Acquisition professionals they work with. This means they are also very responsive and take accountability for their part of the journey.

This shared approach to Talent Acquisition, understanding that the Hiring Manager is responsible for hiring great talent, and Talent Acquisition facilitates the process is the ultimate partnership. You know you have buy-in when they participate in a partnering way, they view your team as the facilitator, and they show shared ownership.

The best part is that the Senior Leadership will then trickle down this confidence in your team through their direct reports, and throughout the organization. They will model the ideal behavior you need to meet your optimized Talent Acquisition function.

There are times when you don't have Executive support that can actually hurt your business. They can impact your Employer Brand, risk compliance issues, or simply create more work for your team. There are some extreme examples as well where the activities of your Executives can actually hinder your ability to attract talent.

At a well-known consumer goods company, their CEO had a very public reputation that was both a positive and negative asset when it came to Talent Acquisition. He had a reputation for being a crazy, wacky innovator who pursued customer satisfaction over anything else. He was also known as a terrible enemy of Human Resources because he didn't believe in the function as a whole. If that's not a downer, I'm not sure what is. This company got some press when an unhappy former employee was interviewed by a national newspaper and the story went viral. The story talked about the company's practices of having peers fire each other, an unsupportive attitude towards Maternity and Paternity leave, and tyrannical yelling from some of the managers. It was not painted as a friendly place to work at all.

That said, of course, the story came from the perspective of someone who felt extremely negative at the time. There were many people who were thriving in that environment, and enjoyed it. While the overall media attention was considered negative – there is an upside to having the culture spotlighted so publically.

A good Human Resources leader can utilize the good with the bad. They use the press, even if it's controversial, to help make sure that the right types of people are interested, and the wrong types are not. From an Employer Brand perspective, bad press can tell certain people that they will not be a good fit at your company and deters them from applying.

At some companies there are a lot of meetings and they like to collaborate in open spaces. This type of environment won't attract people who prefer to work in small offices and spend more time working independently. Your Executive team can help set the tone with this, and get the word out with other Executives. Same could be said for companies who change their policies often. Someone who does not like change should sit this one out!

Executive support is not a myth. I've covered why it's important and what it looks like in good, and bad scenarios in this chapter. If you take anything away from this chapter, it should be that your number one job is to make sure the C-level organization understands that getting and keeping talent should be the number one thing the company does. The Talent Acquisition team should not be the only ones doing this. The Senior Leaders need to play an active role to make this happen. Companies who have a competitive edge will continue to win!

CHAPTER #6

How Should You Best Use Metrics To Monitor The Performance Of Your Talent Acquisition Function?

In the Talent Acquisition world, we love to discuss the idea of measuring our performance. While we all know it's important, many organizations don't do it. Most measure using the metric of 'noise'. Whomever complains the loudest, gets attention when teams are not performing well.

There are many reasons for this, the phrase I hear most often is, "the train keeps moving". Many feel that they don't have the time to develop metrics and measurements. Or it just seems too complex. In some cases, some leaders just don't want to measure their success, because frankly, they are afraid of what the numbers may reveal.

The first step in the metrics game is to go to the business leaders and ask, "How will you measure the success of our Talent Acquisition processes?" Don't just ask the top managers; ask the department managers, supervisors, and unit leaders (i.e., your Hiring Managers). Ask all of them this same question.

Nine times out of ten, they will tell you the two key metrics that matter most are **speed and quality**. Not interview-to-hire ratios, not quality of source, and surprisingly, not even cost.

When Human Resources leaders answer these same questions, they almost always start with cost. But in reality, when you're looking at what's most important overall in increasing the value of the business, Recruiting costs are typically not as important as speed and quality.

It's critical to recognize that if the costs of gathering and presenting the metrics outweigh any possible results that would stem from them, don't waste your time and money. Stop pulling your hair out! This would be the time to admit that someone else's idea of a 'best practice' is not a best practice if it doesn't fit within your own organization. This is where you might want to try a 'success practice', as I shared with you earlier in the book.

In the spirit of ongoing improvement – let's try to anchor on this one thought:

You cannot improve what you don't measure.

Having real-time trend data will allow you to craft some simple, top-level metrics from which the business—not just for your team—will benefit. This is the most helpful approach, and I'll tell you why......

When I was first starting out in Human Resources, I worked for a service company. I was in a job where I was responsible for managing employee benefits and employee safety. I didn't really enjoy the job, but I was good at it.

On the employee safety side, we had to track employee 'lost time' injuries on a report we sent to the corporate office. Every month, our location (one of more than eighty around the world) was ranked on a report that was distributed by the corporate office. If we had more injuries, we ranked lower, and if we had fewer injuries, we ranked higher.

I was constantly under pressure to put together programs and implement systems to move our ranking higher up on that report since our General Manager really cared about the results, and his bonus depended on it. I put programs and systems in place that did work, we saw the results—fewer injuries and happy employees (and happy General Manager, which meant happy me!)

I was then promoted to run all of Talent Acquisition. This role didn't have any reporting requirements - in fact, there were no reports to run at all. I had no real way to prove my success to the corporate office and people outside our little 500-employee location.

I spent hours of my own time on the computer trying to come up with some measurements and metrics that I could use to 'blow my own horn'. I was successful: I came up with all sorts of measurements such as interviews to hire, cost per hire, cost for Recruiting by department, vacancy rate, etc. I spent hours and hours creating reports. Our General Manager was thrilled by these reports and so was I because I could see my results and show success from one period to another. I did so well with this that it got the attention of the corporate office! It led to several more promotions where I got to actually implement nation-wide metrics and measurement programs.

One day I spent some time out in the field with one of our Senior Vice Presidents of Operations. I really wanted to let him know that I was the guy who developed all of those great reports that he received every month. I asked him what he thought of the reports and the data. He said, "I don't read those ridiculous reports, Jeremy! I don't have time for that. Here's the deal: all I care about is getting the best employees we can, as soon as I can get them. Period. All of those reports and work you send— frankly, I don't care. I want results."

A light bulb went off in my head. Measure only what's important to the business and what you intend to use to help you improve your results. Period.

In Talent Acquisition, measuring nothing is obviously not an option. Measuring everything, as I tried to do in my service industry career, is not the answer either. This is where I go back to quality, and speed. You need to be able to evaluate progress, and for that you need metrics that are meaningful, easy to understand, and directly relate to the bottom line. If you're not sure where to start, let's look at two broad categories:

1. Organizational metrics

These are metrics that report what your business leaders tell you is important to them. They are related to the quality of the candidates and new hires and the time it takes to get someone hired, as well as constituent satisfaction. They may therefore be somewhat subjective.

The organizational metrics – which are fewer in number than the efficiency metrics – yield results that the CEO or Senior Vice President would be interested in knowing. But keep reports brief. A good rule of thumb is that if the CEO cannot read and understand your report in thirty seconds, it is too long.

2. Efficiency metrics

These are the types of measurements that you as the Human Resources or Talent Acquisition leader may use to manage internal processes, problems, and issues with methods and systems. These tend to be more objective and numbers-driven metrics, and typically include measuring things such as; individual Recruiter productivity, vacancy/fill rates, sourcing effectiveness, internal cycle times (i.e., how long it takes to present candidates to a Hiring Manager), and certain cost elements.

This information is only important to you as a leader if you can do something with the data. It will help you to identify issues that need correcting and improving, as well as helping to manage your internal performance. These measurements can also be very time-consuming to collect, difficult to analyze, and can be the type of metrics that can make a Recruiting and staffing leader's head spin while he/she is getting those requisitions filled and trying to 'keep the train moving'.

There is a learning curve when it comes to building metrics. The ones that most help the business are going to have to be closely tied to Recruiter accountability. If you are in an environment like I was way back when, and have no metrics, then what you'll quickly learn is that when you try to talk about accountability with Recruiters, the standard fills per month is the worst metric! (A close second worst metric is the time to fill metric).

It does everything possible to incent the wrong behaviors. It means Recruiters are looking to fill roles no matter what, as if filling with just anyone is the right thing to do. Fills per month can be useful for operational guidance, and for a Human Resources or Talent Acquisition leader, it can be helpful to use for resource planning. But if you actually tell a Recruiter they will be measured based on fills per month – driving the absolute wrong behaviors – they will start pushing through bad, lower quality candidates. I strongly suggest adding this to your trash pile.

On the opposite side of the trash pile is the gold: quality metrics. These should be considered the crown jewels of all metrics. If you can measure quality effectively in your organization, you've made it to the top of the mountain.

There are companies out there that attempt to tie the Recruiter to each hire. This could look like a measure on the new employee's performance on the job, their tenure or retention, their ability to be promoted or promotions. Note the differences between *employee quality*, and *quality of hire*. The Recruiter has no ability to impact the employee's performance, and nobody should be accountable for things that are out of their control.

I like to compare quality of hire to an organ transplant. Sometimes, the new heart is a complete match. They took the time to find it, they ran every test possible, and it seemed like a perfect fit. However, even with these conditions, the body can reject the organ and the procedure is a failure. Same thing goes with Recruiting. Sometimes, we find the best candidate, and the Recruiter and the Hiring Manager love them, but then the candidate starts, and the environment rejects them. You quickly see it's not a good fit, and you would never have known that unless you hired them. The environmental issues really make a difference and are out of anyone's control.

I can't recommend quality of hire strongly enough. Let's look at it from another angle. Assume that the Recruiters on your team are having good intake meetings with the Hiring Managers. They are asking for five or six key accountabilities for an open requisition and what the successful candidate will need to achieve in their first year with the company. Sometimes finding someone with the experience, and perceived ability to do the job at hand, is easier and sometimes it's harder. After six months of the successful candidate starting, an Accountant, for example, has to be able to properly reconcile the monthly expenses within five days of the month closing, and within pennies of the balance amount. If the Recruiter does not know that this is what it takes to be successful with this hire, then their questions to the Hiring Manager are not good, and their quality of hire will never meet the mark.

This is why the conversation with the Hiring Manager is so important. Without this information, the Recruiter can only assess what a person has done, and it's not good enough. We need to know what the person can do in the future, and match the past experience to the business' needs. Then you can go back to the Hiring Manager after a period and see if the candidate achieved them, and get a quality rating.

This rating can be applied to the Recruiter to see if they know the accountabilities and they can assess the candidate better based on their resume. A good Recruiter can use phone screens, interviews, and choose the right aptitude exercises to understand what a candidate did similarly and how far a leap the requirements might be. If all parties are aligned to what the business needs them to achieve as an employee, this is the only way to tie the quality of hire back to the Recruiter.

Then, like the organ transplant you can evaluate, within a specific amount of time, if the hire was a successful one. There will always be a Honeymoon period. In some companies, it's three months, in some its 12, after that, the environment will take over and there will either be a good match, or there won't be. Note the sweet spot, one month is too soon, 18 months is too long. Usually, the more junior the role, the faster you will see if the hire was successful based on measurement against what the Hiring Manager asked for. So your call center representatives might take three months to start performing, while roles like Sales, or those in Research & Development could take closer to a year. You'll need to decide what the right amount of time is in order to apply your quality of hire metric properly.

Remember to measure based on the Recruiter, not the new hire. Think about how well the Recruiter gathered information from the Hiring Manager to understand the right fit, and whether or not the new hire is performing against that criteria. Once the decided period of evaluation is over, the Recruiter should not be held accountable for the employee's performance. It's because after this time, the Recruiter has no access to lead or influence the employee. This goes for retention as well, if the new hire works beyond a certain timeframe, and works well, that is where the road ends for your team to influence their contribution to the organization. The same can be said for things like the new hire's performance rating and promotions. In a general sense, these are about team-work, integrity, and customer service, not about the Recruiters ability to place them in the organization.

I once mentored a communications practitioner, let's call him Dan. He was recognized as a top performer at a global technology company and unfortunately landed himself in a situation where the environment rejected him. He was invited to join a telecommunications company to work with an Executive he had once worked for earlier in his career and really respected. Dan figured that since the rapport with the Executive was so strong, that it would be a pleasure to reunite. Dan left the technology company, joined the telecommunications organization and was off to a great start.

Within a few months, Dan was struggling to fit into the cultural norms and conservative pace of the company. Then the Executive Dan joined to work with decided to leave the company. He was left behind without the Executive support he had to soften the cultural differences in the beginning. Many people also affiliated him with the departed Executive, throwing some hostility at him. Dan was certainly not considered a top performer at the telecommunications company. His high output and desire to explore new initiatives were not seen as good things, and he turned out to be a quality hire, who didn't fit.

I won't blow smoke at anyone – measuring quality of hire properly takes a lot of work. It's a muscle to be developed by your team of Recruiters to know how to pull the right information from the Hiring Managers.

The performance of your team is important. While Recruiters work for the love of the Hiring Managers, and take pride in building an organization, you take pride in what the overall function delivers. It's you, the leader of the group, who wants to walk into a room of your peers from across the business and sell, promote, and celebrate all the great work your team is delivering to help the company. You cannot do this effectively if you can't measure, improve, and quantify your success. And do these things in a way that matters to your audience!

CHAPTER #7

*Is Your Leadership Of The Talent Acquisition Function
Inspiring High-Performance?*

Have you ever paused in the middle of the day and wondered why you bother? I have many times, and I feel fortunate that I know the answer to that question. At the heart of it, I am a Recruiter. I build organizations. That is an incredible feat to be part of. And it applies for organizations of all sizes – in smaller ones, each hire makes a huge and immediate impact. In large enterprises, each hire can help the company continue to thrive and look to the future. It seems so simple – **I am a Recruiter. I build organizations**.

If you feel the same way, I hope this shines through for you no matter what. I know as a Human Resources or Talent Acquisition leader, you and your team get beat up often. You get beat up on the number of resumes received, how long it takes to find great candidates, on the cost per hire, and the list can go on and on. What can great leaders take away from this; at the end of the day, you are still building organizations.

Some days you have to dig deeper for the inspiration, but it's well worth it, and your team can easily see the difference. When I started my career as a Recruiter, I quickly learned that it is a thankless job. People spend a lot of time beating you up, directly, and through the Human Resources and Talent Acquisition leadership.

While thankless, I knew that when I walked the halls of the building, I had something to do with so many of the great hires. I took a lot of pride in seeing the smiling faces, hearing the collaboration, and even in the family pictures some employees display in their work spaces. These were great people that I was able to assess and help the business see that they had the skills that would be needed to help our company be successful and continue to make money. So even though I didn't always get a thank you, and even though the Hiring Managers usually took credit for the hire, I knew that I made a difference. I took a lot of slugs, I spent a lot of time convincing someone to come and meet with our team, and convincing the Hiring Manager that the candidate was great.

Through all of this, I knew that in my heart, I did great stuff. Those hallway walks were some of the most enjoyable moments of my busy workdays – they were the little reminders that I was an important part of the team. This is why I was a Recruiter. I had a lot to do with building an organization.

I spent a good amount of time telling you why I am proud to be part of the Talent Acquisition community. I did that because this is the number one reason most people become Recruiters.

You need to know this because as a Human Resources or Talent Acquisition leader, you will need to use this mantra as your drum beat to inspire your Recruiters. I would love to say that this is a group of employees who work to please their direct manager – you. But it's not true. For this unique group, they rarely work for the love of their boss. They work for the love of the Hiring Managers they support, and this is really different from almost all other roles in organizations.

Knowing they may like you and need your guidance, but are really working to win other's hearts, what can you do? There are some other approaches you can take to make sure your team is inspired, high performing, and engaged.

Your role is to lead, motivate, and inspire. However, in the end, the Recruiters don't actually work for you. The work they do is for their Hiring Managers, and they get so few shows of appreciation and love from most of them. It's the dichotomy of the role; they are so closely tied to the success of the Hiring Manager's team, but rarely included in the celebration of achievement. You're not going to change the Hiring Manager's approach most of the time, and it's often fruitless to try – even if you have those stellar relationships we talked about earlier in the book.

Let me share the story of an incredible Human Resources leader who inspired people masterfully. I was working for a consumer brands company and they had a division that produced really cool products. At the time, I was the Head of Professional Staffing for this business group, and did not report into Human Resources. I reported into the business, but of course stayed closely aligned with the Human Resources team and the group's leader, let's call her Lucy. She was a vibrant, passionate person and leader. Even though I didn't report to Lucy, she embraced me as part of her team; I was invited to her team meetings, any activities they planned, and we both considered ourselves part of the same team.

One of Lucy's greatest passions at work was people development. She loved helping the business improve their people development programs, leading proactive succession planning, improving strategic planning processes, working through talent chessboards, and doing talent assessments. She would light up at the start of any discussion she could have with business leaders about any of these areas. Even though she didn't actually do all the work in Human Resources, the people on her team did. She always had endless time and patience to help her team understand how to do things and work on what she was passionate about at the right level. Lucy was deeply invested in their success. She taught them how to achieve the team's goals by guiding and sharing with them so they could soon do this stuff on their own. The results were evident by her team's unbound loyalty and gratefulness to her for helping them grow, have autonomy, and be guided by a master.

Almost rivaling her passion for talent development was Lucy's passion for the company's products. Anything to do with our company's really cool products fascinated her – and she had previously worked for a chemical company – so imagine her delight at coming to our cool company. Everything she did reflected her passion for our products and our brand. Lucy went out of her way to help connect people to how we made money in the industry through our products. She spent time with the people on her team who didn't actually touch production and explained to them how their job impacted the business. From the Benefits Clerk, to the Instructional Designer – they all knew exactly how their role contributed to the business – and they heard it directly from Lucy.

Very sadly, Lucy passed away at a young age – she was just shy of 50. While this is a sad twist of the story, what I wanted to share is how far her passion reached, and the impact she had on people. Her memorial service was held at a large local church that seated over 3,000 people. At Lucy's memorial, it was standing room only. It seemed that everyone she had ever helped had come to pay their respects, and she touched a lot of people. From those she hired, to those she coached, and helped to be successful in their roles, they all came with stories of the inspiring leader she was.

Not all of us can bring the kind of energy and passion Lucy did. Managing people is never easy – especially when your people have several masters. We work with an interesting group of people who are motived in different ways, and by things that are often outside of our control.

Over the years, I've collected some tips that have worked well for me. Many Human Resources and Talent Acquisition leaders get much too focused on processes and keeping the business happy. These things stand in the way of effective of leadership, mentorship, coaching, etc. Our role is often seen as the complaint department. If things don't go right, all the escalations come to you.

If things go right, you often hear radio silence, which we take as an achievement. Of course we know that when you deal with people and process, there are often things that fall off the desired course. You take the feedback like a champion, and many of you deliver it to your employees in a direct and timely way. Of course, this also makes you seem like the grim reaper, the critical scolder, or worse, the scary boss!

A lot of Human Resources and Talent Acquisition leaders fall into this trap. It's a skill to be able to coach, lead, and mentor without being seen as the police, all while connecting with people.

The most important thing I can share with any of you – and while it might seem obvious, I had never put it to words until it really hit me. Hiring and bringing people into an organization is the most emotionally driven thing you do inside a company.

Hiring people is the most important decision in building a successful team. If you make a mistake, it's very visible that you made a mistake. It can follow you for a while. There is a lot of passion and emotion around the organization when you fill a role. Because there is emotion – there are a few things I suggest keeping in mind:

1. **Step Away**. As a leader, you must be able to separate yourself from the emotion. People on your team are responsible to deliver. They may not all react to the same thing in the same way. Since you don't want your office to be seen as the complaint department, you cannot be seen to react to all the feedback that comes in.

Some of it you'll have to take on the chin – don't manage and investigate every comment that comes in. Some of them you shouldn't investigate at all. Which leads me to the next suggestion.

2. **Bucket it.** I've learned the hard way that following up on everything is a lose-lose situation for all. I tried to make myself available to take escalations that came and then run some defense for my team. I did this by bucketing the types of complaints I received, then delivered them to my team in terms of their themes. This way, I didn't single anyone out, and my team could work together at tackling to address these themes. We came up with some great development resources this way. Of course, you'll want to track the complaints, but you can be general with them, for example, responsiveness. I'd share this as a bucketed theme with the team and ask them to share the challenges, what's holding them back, and how we can be better.

3. **Follow the law**. There are cases when things will be emotional, but they must be addressed. If someone tells me something went terribly wrong, for example, someone reported discrimination, or there is a legal risk – I'd have to act. Whether it was unintentional or a gap in process, these are the ones you have to manage specifically, and as they come in.

4. **Set and manage expectations.** We talked about this in terms of relationships with Hiring Managers, and it's important to start with your team. There is a minimum service level required for everyone who is a part of your team. Are they clear on what this level is, and anything outside of those service levels are to

be managed by the Talent Acquisition professionals. They will have their own style and they have to be able to operate in a way that is successful for them and their clients. It's in your best interest to be OK with this, as long as the results are the same at the end of the process.

In Recruiting, there is a difference between high performing, and inspired. High performing means that Hiring Managers, candidates, stakeholders, etc. are generally happy with the service, quality, cost, pipeline that they are receiving from your team.

Inspired means the next level. These would be people who bring a passion for the business and the people they are bringing in. They understand what levers to pull to help the business be successful, and what the future might look like, so they can find talent to meet those needs beyond today. Like Lucy in the consumer brands industry, it's passion mixed with an understanding of the business. This is where people have inspired Talent Acquisition skills.

There is more than one type of inspired leader – and while we can often find similar traits in Recruiters, you as a leader may have another style. I once worked with the Head of Talent Acquisition at a very well-known merchandise company. He could have a 10 minute conversation with a candidate and know if they would fit into the culture and be successful. He knew what it took to get Senior Executives to click well within the organization, and what success looked like. He knew the type of candidate that would help the company to make money and how people could help them succeed or fail. He lived the brand every moment – and was constantly working, simply because he loved it. He loved working with candidates and even spent time talking with spouses about making a change to their company to ensure the full family was on board.

It's about knowing your strengths and weakness and while working to improve, leveraging what you do well to inspire your team. At a technology company that was booming, I worked with two Human Resources leaders. The Talent Acquisition lead was fantastic at storytelling and drawing people in to see and embrace the future. He motivated and excited people and was commonly asked to speak to other groups about the future of the business and tell the story of where the team was going and how the talent his team was looking for would shape the future. Where he had room to improve was in the 1:1 talent development area. Where the rubber hits the road in terms of translating direct performance into meaningful dialogue was a challenge for this leader. He had a hard time helping his team take the vision to a coaching and mentoring level.

His counterpart led Human Resources Strategic programs, like Business Continuity, Relocation, and Compliance – so they worked closely together. This leader was not a very good storyteller. A member of his team once recited to me the rendition he gave of comparing their business to getting the furnace replaced at his vacation house. Now some people would take that story and really make it memorable. This leader got too caught up in the literal story and had many blank stares from people who both didn't own vacation homes, and who would not bother to try and fix their own furnace. Where this leader was excellent, was the 1:1 coaching and helping his team see how their role connected to the bigger picture and the value they brought to the organization.

So whether you soar at the 30,000 foot level, or are the best and most granular leader — realize you will need both to be a great leader.

Whether you're the Human Resources or the Talent Acquisition lead, here are some things you might want to consider asking yourself:

- Are you connecting? Are the conversations between you and your team tying the work you do to how the business will make or lose money?

- Are you acknowledging the day-to-day contributions? Does your team realize on a daily basis how they help the business succeed?

- Have you acknowledged that Recruiting is very emotional for ALL stakeholders? Can you do this from the beginning of each hire, and make sure you are separating yourself if there is a possibility that your influence will cause a significant shift in positive or negative energy. Use this influence to your advantage to get people to perform differently on your team. If people are passionate about one business unit or manager, use that passion and understand what they are excited about to use it with another manager.

- Are you aware of the competition in our world? Talent Acquisition can be managed more effectively than other parts of Human Resources. We can measure so many metrics – from pipeline, satisfaction, time, speed, and cost to name a few. The training team cannot be this granular, nor can benefits, relocation, or technology. This means there is often a competitive spirit within Human Resources, and also between Recruiting teams. Know that this exists and it can allow really great leaders to be able to shift the strategy on communication, and leverage the competition to drive higher performance.

- Are you the only voice of leadership your organization hears? Don't be – it's a lonely place to be. Invite your peers from across the business to talk to your team, or on behalf of your team – internally and externally. Your peers can share what you would have – so you are not the sole leader talking about your team. Internal guest speakers, or a team looking at metrics the same way you do can teach your organization a lot about process. Then you can coach your team to be part of taking on 'best practices', instead of letting them know their current process isn't working. This also helps as Human Resources professionals are often skeptical of each other – an external voice can bring more credibility.

High-performance within a Talent Acquisition team is a tough nut to crack. While you should think about how to inspire your team, be sure that you bring your authentic style to it. Recruiters are some of the best judges of people out there – they can smell a phony from miles away. Your inspiration style should be focused on being your best self, and acknowledging that not all of us can be like Lucy.

CHAPTER #8

Have You Fully Optimized Your Outsourcing Options?

Let's assume you have a high performing team that is inspired. You have Executive support, amazing stakeholder relationships, and your processes and procedures make sense and are compliant. Then the business leader asks you something like, "Why aren't you outsourcing a part of your business, isn't that how Recruiting is done?"

Zap! That one can sting – especially after all your hard work to bring a value added function to the organization.

Human Resources, and Talent Acquisition specifically, have always been the original outsourcers in an organization. It's important to remember that we've used search firms and agencies and third party firms for relocation, and background screening, and to set up contingent and temporary workforces. Ask a typical Recruiting leader and they will likely tell you that they don't outsource their work. Then you give them a gentle reminder, and they realize that they actually do.

There is a real divide between internal and external Talent Acquisition providers. Internal providers have a notion that the reason that they were hired in-house was to do everything an outsourcer would do. They end up taking on way too much work and trying to be everything to everyone.

It's wrong!

Recruiters end up feeling like Samurai soldiers when Hiring Managers ask for all of the items that we referenced above that can be outsourced, the Recruiter feels they have to lay on the so-called sword each time they are asked for this immaculate end-to-end help.

As Human Resources or Talent Acquisition leaders, our job internally, is to get the best talent for the organization. No matter what. It means that we have to make decisions that help us best achieve this goal. If internally we cannot do it faster, cheaper and better than the outside, then we have to acknowledge that there are external experts that can help.

We need to look at the type of job in the first place. For example, in my opinion, in the pharmaceutical industry, the most critical jobs have to do with Research & Development, Commercial and Sales roles, and Manufacturing – that's the list. Everything else that supports a company in this industry, like Human Resources, Legal, Finance, Communication, etc. (staff roles), are on the periphery (again, in my opinion). The roles that touch the product are much more important and critical to the success of the business. Perhaps this view may be the same in your industry? Knowing this, and getting the most effective resources inside focused here is where your team shows the greatest value – both with your internal and external spending.

Ask yourself if your most effective resources are working on these things, and where there is a one-off hire, if your team can handle it. Be realistic about whether an outsourced specialist with a specific core competency can do it better, faster, and cheaper than you can. Outsource what is outside your core competencies so you can focus on what you're good at.

As a Human Resources or Talent Acquisition leader, it's a black hole for you to try and become the Emperor of all Talent Acquisition. Imagine all the jobs, all the levels, all the fluctuation you see in hiring cycles, and even the economy. We all need to have a strong outsourcing strategy that clearly aligns to internal resources to ensure it will be effective. I know many leaders who look at outsourcing as a sword to fall on when they fail. Most important is to first remember that failure can produce a powerful learning moment, if you allow it. And secondly, outsourcing should be part of the overall strategy. Embrace it as part of the bigger picture and make it part of your sales pitch on how your team adds valued services – especially at the core.

There are many considerations to make when finding the best outsourcing strategy for your team. Remember – 'success practices', not 'best practices' apply here too. There have been many developments in the Recruitment Process Outsourcing (RPO) industry over the last few years. If you're not familiar with these organizations, they essentially take all Recruiting functions, and provide these services – from soup to nuts. This can span across sourcing, interviewing, background screening, relocation, hiring and everything in the middle. The difference is that they make it appear that they are doing these tasks from inside your organization.

It sounds logical, doesn't it? The concept initially came out just before the millennium in the late 1990s. It was sold as an amazing idea that someone had come with a flawless process that would make the function better, faster, and cheaper by outsourcing the full process to one company. Industry leaders were told that they didn't need anyone in-house anymore – everything was optimized to make hiring as clear as science.

Not surprisingly, like most things, the RPO firms didn't always deliver. They would create large teams with the latest technology and tools, but to maximize their profits, many of them needed their teams working on different companies at the same time. This meant that their teams could be working on several industries simultaneously. It created conflicts of interest as the candidate pools would span across companies, and unfortunately, shared technology and tools didn't always work for multiple clients. It would often become a square peg, round hole situation.

The more effective business model is to create separate teams that handle each client. It produces better business results, but as with many things that produce better results, they cost more. Full cycle Recruiting going to an outsourced provider means that it can often cost more than keeping the function in-house because your company can now be charged for high overhead costs. The full RPO model went from a proposed golden child, to something that ended up drastically increasing operating costs.

If they become so much more expensive, then why would anyone use an RPO?

There are several reasons to consider RPOs for your organization, even if they end up costing more. It's important to evaluate your strategy to understand where this will be most effective. While they set out to service all areas of Talent Acquisition, RPOs can also be used to work on <u>parts</u> of your business. Some firms don't like it that way, but **they can be very effective in one or two areas** your team has found time consuming. For example, an RPO firm can free up a lot of internal resourcing by taking on sourcing, or developing a pipeline. They could receive a certain number of requisition profiles, and then find the talent for you to fill that roster of candidates. Here are some other reasons you might want to outsource a portion of your business;

- Your **balance sheet** might look better without the internal overhead of the full Recruiting team.

- Your team might be more concerned with **balancing costs over value at the moment. (RPOs can cost much more).**

- You may find value in an RPO firm managing **your non-essential jobs.**

- When you don't want to **focus on non-core jobs**, or need to scale hiring for these roles quickly.

- Your **geography might be larger than the**

resources you have to cover it. RPOs can be used to augment staff for areas that you can't get coverage to.

- You may need help with **candidate coordination** and scheduling.

- Your team might not have the expertise or interest in managing **technology and tools.**

- Your team might want to get a third party to manage parts of the **reference check process**.

- **Social media and social Recruiting** may not be part of your team's core competencies and you're looking for community managers.

- **Candidate assessment** for positions that receive mass amounts of resumes might be an area you need help with.

- Your team may not have the right personalities to connect with candidates on a **university campus**.

Believe it or not, there are several companies who have had difficulties with their campus and university Recruiting programs. Some large companies at one time had experimented with outsourcing all of their campus activities. One in particular was a large retailer. They were proud that they were able to get all related costs off of their P&L (as headcount overhead). The company they outsourced to was a division of a software company – and they were known for their campus process. The software company sold their campus process to many companies, and part of their offering was to represent the company in person on campus. They took this piece on as the retailer was short on resources, so they negotiated a deal for the software company's employees to execute the strategy on behalf of their client. They attended career fairs, campus presentations, and job fairs, but they were not part of the company. As you can imagine, this was not successful. College-age candidates are extremely conscious of the work environment, of authenticity, and the opportunity to be themselves at work. They quickly found the software provider disingenuous. They had no experience working at the client's company, and had never lived in the city the company was headquartered in. It was a terrible experiment – and the client learned from it – quickly.

We're all on the same page on this – everything we do as leaders has to show a good return on investment. If your business is against outsourcing, your job is to show what the business case is, and the bottom line of what kind of value will come back to the company if they invest.

I spent some time working for a large global client and when I started, they had outsourced their entire Recruiting process to several global RPO firms. They didn't have the appetite to add headcount, or any sort of G&A work on the P&L. They REALLY didn't want to see it on their books. So they kept it as a variable cost. Many of their business leaders liked the way it looked, and many thought they were saving money.

When we looked at the costs together – and I mean really looked at them – we found that they were paying way more versus what they were actually getting. It looked something like this; the RPO had 3.5 people working on the business in a specific geographic market, for a cool $1.5M per year. The business leaders were surprised they were spending this much, and they didn't even know it because it wasn't their headcount.

For that kind of money, we showed the business that they could hire at least 6 full time hires, possibly close to 10 for the exact same money. Their CEO asked questions that are common when considering bringing a function back internally – what about the cost to keep full time hires on board, and what about the effort and risk if we need to fire them?

This is where your strategic analysis matters the most. In the end the cost-value has to pan out. I've given you a few examples, and what I've seen in my experience is that we should be calling RPO, 'Faux PO'. Or maybe 'RP-No'.

Some RPO firms sell their value by saying that they will do all Recruiting. They sign contracts, then hire contingent staff themselves as your new Recruiters.

They post your roles online, then pay these employees only 60-70% of what they charge you. Their new hires have no experience, and no relationships. The RPOs are essentially the broker of contingent staff. Something that you can also easily set up yourself internally, but without the markup.

When you offload this labor, you are truly getting nothing more than contingent staff. They have no connection with the team, they're missing that 'mojo' that makes internal teams so successful. They have no process expertise, the very thing they sold you on earlier. And yet, they continue to sell the idea that they have a unique proprietary methodology to make things more effective.

Much like the Wizard of Oz, when you pull the curtain back on what you think is the great and powerful Oz, what many realize is that it's a fake reality. Some RPOs are not really providing a true system, process, or methodology. Check it out and ask good questions.

Personally, I don't give away core responsibilities. Like the story I told you earlier about the service organization that used an RPO model, their candidate experience suffered. As soon as candidates wanted to know about the location, manager, or anything specifically related to the company, the relationship unraveled because members of the RPO team were not prepared to answer these questions. They can only engage in a one-way discussion that helps them check boxes and fill in responses through their strict processes. This is not good. That client eventually had to bring the function back in-house.

There are cases when your business leadership will be very supportive of outsourcing. They may even try to push you to use one for areas that are working well internally. These are the moments to assert your strategic value in a balanced way. I'll take you back to the importance of return on investment and a side by side comparison of cost will almost always yield the result of the RPO model being much much much more costly – and lacking the added value your internal resources can bring to the organization.

Remember to think about this; the RPO cannot be offloaded as a transaction. Its very relationship driven, and we all know well, that in our business, it's all about relationships. The benefit of the internal Recruiter-candidate experience is that they can speak to what it's like to work at that company. How many candidates ask about the workplace culture, experience, and managers they might one day work with? How might that feel to them if they aren't speaking to people who can answer this from experience?

This is food for thought for you. If you've worked so hard to gain internal credibility, what might happen when you outsource the core? When you outsource the core, it's easy to lose the value of Talent Acquisition. Not all jobs are core to the business, even though every hire contributes to the success of the company. You may not be saving any money either – how do you sell that one?

As we close off this chapter, know that I am not against RPOs. I think there is a lot of value in offloading the work that is outside of your core. I would urge you to be strategic about where you outsource, and what you outsource. It has to be a real strategy. RPOs are not the worst at all, and you can save yourself a lot of time and money if you don't make the wrong assumption that they are the panacea.

CHAPTER #9

How Do You Ensure You Have A Consistently Great Candidate Experience?

Your Employer Brand is strong – we covered that earlier in the book, and let's assume your aspiration is accurate for today's reality of your company. Now let's put the rubber to the road – is everyone at your company contributing to a consistently great candidate experience?

One of the things I've learned over the last few years is that the candidate experience is becoming more and more important. I've done a lot of benchmarking in this area, and we've gathered a lot of information, and discovery. What we've learned is that what candidates actually have to say about a client's company is not anywhere near what the company thought. While sometimes shocking, and tough to swallow, it is extremely helpful. This is because many organizations don't bother to ask candidates about their experience. Or they might only ask a part of the candidate pool, say, those who received an offer. They may at times also ask the people who turned down an offer once it was made, but very few ask <u>all</u> the candidates about their experience (especially those that are rejected). You can learn a lot by being inclusive on this front.

During this benchmarking process, we're looking to learn why the experience is mixed or not good. In many cases, it's because there are no clear guidelines for what an acceptable candidate experience really is. Some organizations have a blanket understanding that an experience is effective if certain basic things happen. For example, if you don't make people sit and wait without a bathroom or eating break for hours on end.

Even within the same company, you could have one department that does something totally different than others, and equally unpleasant for candidates because there are no clear candidate guidelines or 'bill of rights'. There is no clear set of guidelines that everyone had to agree to follow so that the team will be successful. Some of these guidelines might be things like; the candidate will not have to come to the office more than three times, or they will not be expected to interview right when they land from a red-eye flight, or they will never wait more than 20 minutes without contact with an employee while they are on your premises.

When you are missing a set of candidate care guidelines, you will always have inconsistency. A 'bill of rights' is a simple way to improve the experience. Think of it this way, each team is special so they should be able to do their own things; but all candidates should be treated the same, right?

If your company's culture is to be one of optionality

for all things you would never accomplish anything standardized. In reality, a culture where there is too much optionality tends to end up operating much like the federal government and state governments in the US. I'm sure many of us can appreciate that this was not the intention of having 50 united areas – to have them operate in a drastically different way. A company can be viewed in the same way. No matter what it is, your company's brand should present the same experience and feel no matter what the encounter, and not doing this can be detrimental.

Put yourself in the shoes of a candidate. You're interviewing with one company that makes you jump through hoops. They might feel that if you can conquer their hoops, then you will be suitable to work there. However, as a candidate in a competitive market where companies are looking for top talent, and having to compete for it, you as the candidate can easily walk away not interested in the company, or their products after a bad experience.

Your company needs your help to see this! I recently worked with a client who pushed back hard on the recommendations I gave based on the benchmarking process I took them through. They didn't believe the candidates were that unhappy. I had to give them a dose of reality and read over 100 quotes from candidates who had subpar experiences, and the business leaders were stunned. It spurred them to do something quickly when they saw that the experience candidates were having was going viral on social media, and it was not flattering to their brand at all. They took the discovery and benchmark information and they decided to use it. After a lot of 'this is important' and C-level conversations, they agreed to put together a candidate care charter, an implementation plan, and a training plan. They landed in a good position to fix their candidate experience that impacted their Employer Brand by not just planning to make a change, but mapping out how to implement it as well.

Every time you interact with a candidate, you create an impression. When the process is over the candidate may walk away thinking, "Wow, what a great company - if they had another opening I'd apply there again." Or the candidate may think, "What a bunch of jerks. I'd never want to work there." Now multiply these impressions dozens or even hundreds of times. This is a powerful force. This is your professional brand, and part of your Employer Brand.

By definition, branding is a means of identifying and differentiating a company, a product, or a service.

Branding includes the tangibles and intangibles, features, services, and benefits that create and influence an ongoing relationship. It is the development of an affinity for a product that in turn takes on elevated meaning and a predisposition to buy or join.

This is a HUGE competitive advantage for your brand and greatly helps your efforts attracting the top talent that is so competitive to find today.

The candidate experience is not a 'nice to have'. You simply can't ignore it and expect to be successful. Know that in one area, this one area to be exact, you have no choice. With every candidate interview you are creating your brand; you just may not be managing your brand. You are communicating who you are and what it will be like to work for your organization. It also speaks to the people already working for you. Internal interviews are equally important as you manage how people feel when they leave an interview.

I suggest starting with a high level of professionalism and ethics in how you interact with your individual candidates. Don't forget about the candidates you do not hire as well, they still matter greatly. Think about how you interact with the company and its Executives and Hiring Managers.

You live in a 360-degree world of relationships. As a Human Resources or Talent Acquisition leader, you need to set the example for creating and nurturing positive relationships with stakeholders including; your pool of job candidates, Human Resources Generalists in your company, Hiring Managers, and third-party Recruiters. Some of these relationships may seem competitive or even adversarial; in others, you hold power that you must use wisely. In every case, openness, high ethical standards, and a positive attitude will help you build your personal brand and enhance your career. This is before you actually even interact with candidates.

I've had the privilege of working for a variety of clients in more industries than I'd ever imagined. Let me share with you some of the 'success practices' I've seen for creating a great candidate experience.

Tailor to each candidate pool. You know well that different types of roles can result in different types of candidates. While no two are ever alike, you can tailor the experience based on what you know about each group. This might be as simple as different pages on your website, or using technology tools in specific ways.

Tailor to each culture/country. Some cultures add a lot of personal information to resumes and CVs, and some are much more impersonal. Recruiting practices and norms vary from country-to-country and region-to-region. There is no 'one size fits all.' Thus understand what makes the Recruiting culture unique in each country or region that you work and customize your approach to address those needs.

Tailor your technology to each culture/country. Remember each country or region may have its own unique tools to identify where the candidates you seek are lurking. Thus it's important to know some of the specific gathering places. Your social media pages are so important to your Employer Brand and is often the starting point for your candidate experience.

While global differences matter greatly, there are some things that every company can look into. These are the tried and true tips that apply to all organizations around the world:

Train your Hiring Managers. We talk about the need to help your Hiring Managers be good partners. They can benefit from your expertise in this area too. Identify where people in your organization can benefit from coaching and guidance on how to interact with candidates and ensure the expectations are clear to them.

Encourage employee referrals. There is no better advocate for your company than someone who already loves working there. Some company's programs were scaled back during to the economic downturn but their time is returning and it's important to continue to actively promote these programs and ensure that they have a positive image and reputation that is marketed well internationally and companywide.

Put your job descriptions in your company's voice. Gone are the days of the boring job descriptions – or so they should be. Telling your company story comes from so many places. It's a huge missed opportunity to have a fantastic website and Employer Brand and have job descriptions that make people yawn. The right key words and searchable terms are vital to attract the type of people with the required skills and experience. Ask the people currently excelling in the role how they would describe the job.

Customize strategies for different regions. Whether you are part of a global operation, or a national one, you need to develop and maintain a separate strategy for each region, taking into consideration local customs and idiosyncrasies. Think about a meeting in Plano, Texas, compared to one in Cambridge, Massachusetts. You can imagine the differences, even if you haven't lived in these cities. While Talent Acquisition is best done by region, sourcing teams that work by channel will be the most successful. Allow sourcing teams to become Subject Matter Experts in multiple regions so they can build a strategy and identify the competitive landscape. Address each channel separately, one at a time, until you identify how best to reach and communicate with local talent.

Imagine how a candidate will feel if you can help them make connections with locals who know things like:

- What are the top schools?

- How do parents register their children and when?

- What is the local housing market like?

- Which areas might young single people live in if they move close by?

When talking with people from other cultures, remember that they might consider direct solicitation to be rude, or they may be unsure how to react or respond to direct approaches. Here are a few examples I learned about over the years that greatly determined the candidate experience:

Germany. Online searches in German yield much better results. Direct Recruiting tends to be viewed negatively. Email response is relatively high. Germans are comfortable with direct personal questions during a phone interview.

Netherlands and Denmark. Recruiters from the outside this region need to make sure they probe firmly for package details of Dutch candidates, who will typically tell you what they expect to earn, not what they currently earn. Part of the deal negotiation with Danish candidates can be how many newspapers and magazine subscriptions the company will pay for—much to the incredulity of the UK and US Recruiters!

Australia. People from this country respect others with strong opinions, even if they don't agree, so state your point clearly. Direct phone calls work best. Prospects are very approachable, but are used to working through agencies.

South Africa. Direct email response rate is low. Prospects respond better via introductions from gatekeepers.

South America. US-based Recruiters - do not let your team members be offended if they are called 'Gringos'. South Americans use this term to refer to people from the United States, and it is not meant to be insulting. Don't expect Executive-level candidates to be on resume databases or social networks; it may be seen as a sign of them looking for a job, which is a no-no.

United States. Some Americans often share things in casual conversation, even with strangers, which may seem shockingly private.

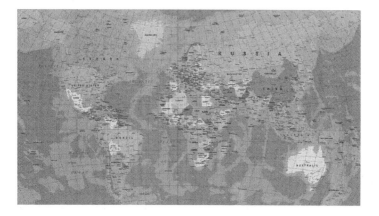

Now that you've thought about your approach from the inside out, let's talk more about the candidate's point of view. How can you know if you've done a good job with candidates? Are you sure that they're walking away from each encounter with your organization with positive thoughts?

How about you start by asking them about their experience. Yes, I said it! I'm not sure why so many people are afraid to speak to candidates about their experience. Perhaps some time back in 1965, someone said "Don't talk to the candidate" and it seems everyone has been afraid since then. What would happen if you asked some questions in a consistent way, perhaps did a survey, then followed up with the same questions each time.

This would likely yield you a baseline of consistent themes from the survey and conversations. If you do this over a period of time, you'll have a place to measure from – how great! Without this information, do you know what the candidates are feeling? You can use this information to ensure you know how you should treat people, and be able to set up guidelines.

Some of the things my clients have learned about in the past by using this method have been things like expenses. Candidates didn't appreciate having to pay for expenses from their own pocket to travel to interviews. They shared that the reimbursement process was either very slow, or they never received their money back.

Another candidate experience that many don't appreciate is when we invited them in to do multiple interviews, and ask them to do more than four in one day. While our Hiring Managers often appreciated the opportunity to complete all interviews in one day, the candidates told us it was a long and draining day, and they often didn't have breaks scheduled.

A client used this feedback to take over all logistics, so they paid for them upfront making their travel budget more predictable, and adjusted their schedule to ensure candidates had an hour break at some point during multiple interviews. They also ensured all candidates would hear from the Recruiter within a specified amount of time. It would be to share feedback or provide a status update.

Even with a consistent experience recorded, your candidates could face interactions, from an incredible experience to a very poor one. Where do you want it to be?

It's often difficult to start from the inside out. Many times, I've started working with clients in this area as an objective third party. Some organizations are afraid of what they might learn when they ask candidates how their experience was. It is truly the only way to know once a candidate leaves your premises.

In 2008, right before the financial crisis in the US, I was working with a company Time Magazine named 'The fastest growing company in the world'. They hired me to help them re-position their transactional Recruiting organization, into a strategic Talent Acquisition team. In addition to our evaluation of current practices, we surveyed over 500 candidates that had interviewed in the past 6 months to understand what they liked, and what they found lacking.

Using the baseline from the surveys, we developed an eight step guide on how to work with candidates. Everything was in there from the first phone call, to the offer or decline. We trained the Recruiters to follow it, and then empowered them to work with the Hiring Managers to socialize and train them. It was a success case that the team found very useful and helped the Talent Acquisition team build relationships with evidence from candidates to anchor why we had to do things a certain way.

When I worked with another large company, we did an assessment of their organization. They had a wonderful Project Manager working with them and we spent a week working through a presentation about their candidate experience. In the Human Resources leader's nervousness about the results, they spent cycle after cycle evaluating the font size and changing bullet colors. They spent a lot of time warning me to be careful when we presented – they didn't feel their team would be prepared to hear the candidate feedback.

The feedback was not great. Candidates had negative feedback about the slow reimbursement process for travel expenses. They also thought the business was very slow in giving candidate feedback and even closing the loop when they weren't going to move forward in the interview process. I was able to deliver this information without emotion to the Human Resources leader and the Executive team – they had an easier time hearing my accusation-free report that was based on empirical data. I would want the same thing if the roles were reversed, and I think it's why I've done a lot of these exercises!

Once you have this data, make sure you transform your team from the inside out. Like the candidate experience guide I mentioned earlier – your team has to be on the same page. Sometimes it's even harder to get your team around this bend than it is to get the leadership team to see the challenges. We used the guide as a tool to give Recruiters pride in the experience they were creating. We used the next round of surveys showing the improvement and took the time to celebrate the team's success in creating a greatly enhanced candidate experience.

If you're not sure where to start, I recommend mapping out the process you have today. Then using results from candidate feedback mechanisms, use that data, along with your public profile from sites like Glassdoor.com.

These will give you a good baseline to manage against. Hear me when I tell you that you will *never* be able to control all the personalities around you. You'll need to know how to use your relationships with your Hiring Managers to coach them to be able to join efforts to create an experience that leaves candidates salivating at the chance to join your team. Be sure to keep things consistent – every experience should start with the same intention, even if things will happen that could go wrong along the way.

As Human Resources and Talent Acquisition leaders, it's our role to ensure the candidate experience aligns with the Employer Brand. We are in the business of not only finding the right person to occupy a role, but to remember that the human being we recruit has dreams, aspirations, and cultural beliefs that may be deeply cherished. The candidate wants to be welcomed into the organization as a friend and colleague, and not be made to feel as though they are suddenly working among strangers.

While you may not achieve the 'Cheers' level where 'everyone knows your name', it is important to be intentional about your candidate experience. Be sure to map out a fantastic, repeatable, measurable experience, then help everyone at your company ensure you can bring it to life.

CHAPTER #10

*Is Your Team Nimble And Flexible Enough To Change
With Minimal Resistance?*

The late American poet and civil rights activist, Maya
Angelou one said "If you don't like something, change
it. If you can't change it, change your attitude." This is
interesting because it's so relevant, and seems so simple.
We all know that this is not the case though. It's your
team's job to create and deliver a great experience, but
what happens if they don't like change?

Is it an uphill battle every time you need to make an
adjustment? Does your team resist to the point that it's
difficult to be agile? Can you feel the frost come over
them when you try to propose an improvement?

Of all of the issues that are discussed amongst our circles,
communities, and at conferences, the one that I find
most important is rarely discussed. It's that hot topic of
leading and managing change. This skill is probably one

of the most important a Human Resources or Talent Acquisition leader should have in their toolkit.

In our communities, we're constantly coming up with and discussing great ideas about initiating change, but all of that is worthless unless we can execute and implement those ideas. We have to change and flex every minute of the day, planning for difficult times and good times alike require excellent change management skills. Take it from someone who has learned some hard lessons over the course of my career – I didn't always know how to manage change either.

For instance, when I was head of staffing for a large, multi-billion-dollar company, the whole company participated in a global reengineering initiative. In Human Resources, we decided to take advantage of this effort to implement some changes of our own. We were going to combine all of the staffing functions in the separate business units into a centralized, shared-services model. As the leader of the staffing area, I figured that since the whole company was going through change, there was no need to have any additional communication with our clients about our staffing reorganization—after all, it could be simply considered another element of what we were all going through.

It wasn't until one of my peers in Human Resources and my boss were sitting in my office, complaining about my team's dwindling performance in the wake of this change that I realized just how important it is to communicate extensively about, and have a comprehensive plan for, implementing change.

It's not that I didn't communicate at all about what was

happening; it's that I didn't 'get it' in terms of what was necessary with respect to engaging others and making them partners with me in this change. I was subjecting my plan to what we like to call 'Death By PowerPoint.' I was going around with my little PowerPoint presentation tucked under my arm, informing everyone as to what was going to happen versus truly engaging and communicating with them. Though the change was ultimately implemented, the cost was high—people we wanted to keep within our staffing organization left and some of our customers were alienated.

It's not enough to adopt a popular Global Change Management Program. For each change you need to have a specific change plan and internal and external change communications plans. Without those in place, not only is it confusing for everyone but it totally kills your high-performance, inspired team momentum, and ends up costing the company money.

I'll say it again as I've had to repeat it in person many times. **Each change needs its own plan**. I learned this quickly; after a tough lesson. I figured our change would be part of the larger change plan, I did not feel the need to create a separate one for us in Talent Acquisition.

An effective change management plan will focus on many levels, the broad as well as the specific, and will include an emphasis on everything from the organization, to your team, to individuals. In fact, the act of putting together the plan will be enormously helpful because it will not only require identifying who the stakeholders are and who will be affected, but it will also require strategizing about how to approach and engage them in the implementation.

Importantly, having a plan will enable you to plan for mistakes, which is a vital and valuable part of any new venture. How will a plan give you the opportunity to make mistakes? Because the cornerstone, foundation and lifeblood of any change management plan is perhaps the most vital element in the whole change management scenario: communication.

A communications strategist I once worked with shared with me the battle she faced. The organization was making people changes which would have a ripple effect on the Talent Acquisition team and process. She came to the table armed with change management plans and a strong communication background – which was normal for her. In the wake of the changes though, one of several risk-averse stakeholders, Media Relations, wanted to kill the planned communication to key parts of the business. They debated the merits of cutting off communication to what they called, 'groups outside the core', to minimize potential leaks to the media and keep the impact under wraps.

Trying to be a collaborator, our communications strategist painted a picture of what would happen if the information was not shared with all impacted groups. You can imagine what this looked like. Not only was it difficult to rebuild organizational trust, but the stakeholders, like Talent Acquisition would continue full speed down the wrong path without this information being shared with them proactively. She lost that battle, and of course won the war, which became much more of a crisis than it needed to be. In the end, the full communication plan was executed and the change was adopted. It only took eight months longer and cost the business $2.5M more than planned though.

Engaging people from the very beginning is so important. Imagine a scenario in your organization – one that needs some sprucing up. What would happen if you started out by using focus groups? You'd not only get people involved who are going to be affected and share your vision and proposed process, but they would help you figure out how to really make it work. It is critical to engage stakeholders and then communicate, monitor and adjust your process continuously. It's a constant process of educating Hiring Managers, Human Resources partners and key business leaders and getting feedback.

When communicating, try to mix it up and remember the importance of storytelling as a medium to share information. It's not only easier for you to seem more natural in delivering a story, but it's more entertaining and memorable for your audience too.

During your focus group meetings, consider using interactive voting devices to keep the audience engaged in answering questions and giving feedback. There are so many incredible tools out there now that will boost interaction in meetings, and give you invaluable feedback. You can even rent some of these tools by the hour!

In your rollout of the new process, make a video showing changes you're trying to make and focus on the 'why' you're doing it. Can you deliver it with some humor as well to keep it fresh, or connect it to something familiar and positive? Perhaps you can create a contest using your enterprise social media platform and publically recognize and reward those who support the changes by participating. You can also use a 'Myth Of The Month' whereby you debunk the latest 'myths' that have surfaced with respect to the new processes. Through the use of Hiring Manager and candidate surveys, you can constantly monitor to determine what is or isn't working properly, and then adjust accordingly.

But sometimes, even that level of communication isn't enough. You know that old rule of when you pack for a trip, you lay out all your clothes and then take away half? Change management communication is the opposite of that. No matter how much you plan to communicate with respect to change management, you should take that plan and double it.

Why is this important? Whatever the change is you're implementing, it's not about it being good or having the right idea, it's about bringing everyone along with you. One of the things people in staffing management often don't understand is communications is not just about making sure you and your ideas are heard, it's about making sure everyone is with you. It's a bit of a paradox: in order to do what you want to do, you need to focus less on that and more on the communication needs of those affected. Because in the end, that will help you get to where you want to go. You need to focus on what your clients and stakeholders need to hear and know so that they'll arrive at where you want them to be.

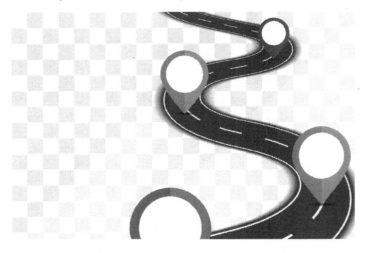

This approach underscores yet another mistake I made in my scenario from earlier. I was so focused on communicating my change and ensuring I was heard that I didn't focus on the communication needs of my clients and stakeholders.

When it comes to managing change, there is nothing more important than communication. And as with a change management plan, constant communication gives you the room to make mistakes.

It feels uncomfortable to lead through change in the beginning. Don't allow others' doubts to sway how you will lead your organization. If you truly believe that you are doing the right things, then make sure everyone around you knows that. If your start is a little rockier, here are some guidelines for leading people through change:

» Prepare for the change before it occurs.

» Provide a clear description of the change and a picture of success.

» Find and remove obstacles before the change occurs.

» Allow adequate time for people to accept the change.

» Involve affected people in planning the change.

» Provide motivation for people to embrace the change.

» Find and utilize resources and people that support the change.

» Allow the change to be shaped by ongoing feedback.

» Provide clear implementation objectives for all people involved in the change.

» Continually monitor the change and adjust resource levels.

» Reinforce the new behaviors through formal and informal methods.

» View leading others through change as an ongoing process.

Remember, though there are a thousand great ideas out there, only when you've developed a plan, and successfully executed on that plan will you have developed perhaps the most important skill there is to improve your value in your organization.

Change can come from within your organization, but just as often it is imposed from the outside environment, such as during a recession.

There's no question the global recession of the later part of the first decade of the 21st century was difficult and a game changer for Recruiters. Not only did Human Resources and Talent Acquisition leaders have to take a serious look at scaling down their operations, but after the markets rebounded, many teams never fully staffed back up to the initial glory. The reason for this is that we didn't need as many as before.

While inevitable during tough times, many Human Resources Generalists became much more sophisticated about staffing.

After the economic downturn began, people in these roles were forced to pick up the slack. They learned to be better Project Managers and more open to hiring additional resources, such as outsourced providers and search firms. And because they were closer to the business than their former Recruiter colleagues, as the economy continued to improve companies didn't need as many Recruiting Specialists, and those Recruiting jobs that did return didn't pay as much.

What was made clear is that we, as leaders in the Talent Acquisition world, have to survive and prosper through a downturn and as recovery begins.

So getting back to change – you may notice that there are some specific things that you'll need as an individual, and other things that you'll need to prepare your team. Keep in mind that the two should work hand in hand

– remember, if you don't believe in the changes you are making, how can you expect your team to follow?

The basic principles are the same for managing change for individuals, teams, and organizations. For individuals, for example, you might ask your Recruiters to follow a procedure of implementing Hiring Manager intake meetings on every new search, where they did not have to before. They can react in a variety of ways, but will generally get on board with your support and the value they get back from the task.

For your team, perhaps they will have to implement new metrics that measure their own performance against a goal, where in the past there were just anecdotal metrics.

An organization may have to drastically change its structure, reporting relationships, and whole jobs (titles, functions, and reporting relationships) along with its processes and outputs.

Employees will move through change at different rates. Your ongoing role is to help employees embrace the change and influence future behavior. Encourage employees to discuss their concerns; be prepared to listen. Display confidence in the company and in leadership. It is critical that you as leaders help your employees through the change. All change, whether good or bad, does cause some angst. We must provide our employees opportunities to question and internalize the change, and then focus the team on the business goals and objectives. The role of the leader is to help your team members understand the change, embrace the change and then focus on the future.

Have you ever wondered if you were effective in the changes you've had to make? What about any collateral damage of the change – perhaps your execution was flawless, but you lost a lot of organizational trust, or it was a rocky road, but really ended up bringing your team together?

"It turns out we don't know the definition of change."

I suggest measuring in three key areas; thinking, feeling, and doing.

Thinking. We assess the current state. Where are we today? Why do we need to change? Who will be impacted (stakeholders)?

We define the future state. Where do we need to go? What will success look like (metrics)? What are the obstacles?

We formulate the rationale for the change. We create a team to execute the plan and we make sure Senior

Leadership and key stakeholders buy-in.

Remember to stay clear about your expected outcomes.

Feeling. We communicate value. We share the business case, share the plan for how success will be achieved, and ensure understanding of individual's roles and how they will be evaluated.

The goal is to gain and increase stakeholder commitment. To do this we develop solid communication plans for all key stakeholder groups and involve stakeholders early on. We consider the personal and professional impacts to key stakeholders and address them.

Doing. Change must not be merely discussed and planned, but implemented. We need to ask ourselves how we will change the way we do our work. How are we going to know the change has been implemented? How are we measuring the change (using the metrics established)? What accountabilities are in place? And how will resources be adjusted?

Change is an ongoing process. It's not something to start and back out of – you will lose your credibility if this happens too often. Your commitment to change must be sustained. New behaviors must be recognized and reinforced, and we need an ongoing communication plan.

We need to assess organizational impacts in areas including compensation, training, the governing model, operating mechanisms, and metrics.

And after all these things are done, think about the

moments after the 'touchdown'. How are you celebrating the success of the change? Is your team feeling fatigue and do you know what the signs are inside your organization?

Never forget that you are a change agent. Many Human Resources and Talent Acquisition leaders before you learned significant lessons to help us arrive at this notion! You will work on some truly inspirational changes in your time; ones that make you feel as if you'll conquer the world. Others might be really difficult, like downsizing a team you hand-selected from employee number one.

Don't let fear stop you from doing a great job at leading through change. From being someone that people want to follow because you have a clear vision, you communicate clearly, and you always bring others along on your journey.

You need to be your own leader and support what you believe in. If you don't, nobody will.

CONCLUSION

When you picked up this book, you might've had a mild curiosity about what someone who specializes in helping organizations develop stronger internal Recruiting and staffing capabilities might have to say. I hope you've enjoyed this short read, but more importantly, that you've had a few moments where you stopped and considered. Perhaps you thought to yourself "Am I leading a high-performance Talent Acquisition team?"

I'm not suggesting you're not at this moment, but let's face it, there is always a lot of movement for a Human Resources or Talent Acquisition leader. And through all the movement, I know that you really want your team to be the best they can possibly be at sourcing, attracting and hiring top talent into your organization.

In a global talent landscape that is now the most competitive it has ever been, your responsibilities and importance to your organization have become critical to its growth and competitiveness.

At times it can be difficult for people in our field to connect. There may be candidates, or candidate pools that you and someone you would otherwise connect with, are both fishing in. You might find it difficult to step outside your organization to learn about 'success practices', or you might be facing an uphill battle without Executive support.

It's all to say that Human Resources and Talent Acquisition leaders are some of the most passionate and hardworking people I have ever met. And this is what makes you great at your role. You fight through, you persevere, and you use your crystal ball as best you can (with your deep understanding of your business of course!) to build organizations.

I hope you've had the light bulb go off a few times throughout this read, and that perhaps some of the 'success practices' might resonate at your company. I hope that some of the chapters made you question plans you have in place, perhaps your RPO, or how you influence your Employer Brand. Perhaps you will question some plans you don't have in place, but should, like a solid change management approach, or a candidate experience guide.

In a hyper competitive market as we are in today, none of us can afford to miss out on great talent because of a Talent Acquisition function that is not optimized. And let's face it, we all want to come to work each day and be around inspired, hard-working, and strategic colleagues.

Your quest to give your team the best tools so they can be successful day after day matters. It's the difference between winning and losing.

I've spent over 25 years helping organizations move from the losing side, to the winning side, and I love what I do. I truly hope that the insights and strategies that I have learned working with our global clients help you gain that edge that you are looking for.

If this book resonates with you and you'd like a Complimentary Talent Acquisition Strategy Session (Value $1495.00) to discuss how to optimize your Talent Acquisition function to reach your objectives and benchmarks, then reach out to my office at +1-562-856-5787 or visit www.RivieraAdvisors.com/StrategySession

Wherever you are in your Talent Acquisition journey, I sincerely hope that you continue to reach for the stars – that is, of course, figuratively, and in the top talent you are looking for.

INDEX

A
Applicant Tracking System (ATS), 5–6, 9, 10
asset assessment, 27

B
best practices vs. success practices, 4–6, 8, 49, 73
branding. See Employer Brand

C
campus and university recruiting programs, difficulties
    with, 76–77
campus strategy for success in hiring, 39
candidate experience
    author experience with candidate surveys, 93–94
    clear candidate guidelines, necessity of, 83
    cultural expectations, 87, 89–90
    Employer Brand, impacting, 25, 85, 86, 95
    feedback, soliciting, 91–94